W9-BIP-444

WITHDRAWN

THE CALMS OF CAPRICORN

EUGENE O'NEILL

The Calms of Capricorn

A PLAY

Developed from O'Neill's Scenario

by Donald Gallup

With a Transcription of the Scenario

TICKNOR & FIELDS

New Haven and New York

1982

Copyright © 1981 by Yale University

All rights reserved. No part of this work may be reproduced or trans-
mitted in any form or by any means, electronic or mechanical, including
photocopying and recording, or by any information storage or retrieval
system, except as may be expressly permitted by the 1976 Copyright Act
or in writing by the publisher. Requests for permission should be addressed in writing to Ticknor & Fields, 383 Orange Street, New Haven,
Connecticut 06511

CAUTION: Professionals and amateurs are hereby warned that *The
Calms of Capricorn,* being fully protected under the copyright laws of the
United States of America, the British Empire, including the Dominion
of Canada, and all other countries of the copyright union, is subject to a
royalty. All rights, including professional, amateur, motion picture, tele-
vision, recitation, public reading, radio broadcasting, and the rights of
translation into foreign languages, are strictly reserved. All inquiries
regarding this play should be addressed to Yale University, c/o Cad-
walader, Wickersham & Taft, One Wall Street, New York, NY 10005.

The Eugene O'Neill Collection was founded at the Yale University
Library in 1931 by Carlotta Monterey O'Neill. It includes notes, photo-
graphs, and the manuscripts of plays, among them *The Calms of Capricorn.* All royalties from the sale of this book go to Yale University for
the Collection of American Literature, for the purchase of books in the
field of drama, and for the establishment of Eugene O'Neill Scholarships
in the Yale School of Drama.

Library of Congress Cataloging in Publication Data

O'Neill, Eugene, 1888-1953.
  The calms of Capricorn.

  I. Gallup, Donald Clifford, 1913-   II. Title.
PS3529.N5C34   1982   812'.52   82-715
ISBN 0-89919-093-6   AACR2

Printed in the United States of America

V 10 9 8 7 6 5 4 3 2 1

CONTENTS

INTRODUCTORY NOTE

The Calms of Capricorn was the original starting point for the cycle of plays in which Eugene O'Neill planned to trace the fortunes of an American family, the Harfords, and the effect upon them of the corrupting power of material things. This "Clipper Ship-around-Horn" play had grown out of his fascinated interest in the romantic ships that sailed the seven seas for a short but glorious period in the mid-nineteenth century. At Château Le Plessis on 12 May 1930, Carlotta Monterey O'Neill noted in her diary that "Gene [is] reading book on 'Clipper Ships,'" and in Paris on 6 August 1930 she wrote that he "buys marvellous books on Clipper Ships." O'Neill was then hard at work on the third draft of *Mourning Becomes Electra.* As he was completing the sixth and final draft, Carlotta reported, on 16 March 1931, that he "discusses writing Clipper Ship play next!" Three months later, on 20 June, he actually set down in his notebook his "Clipper Ship-around-Horn" idea:

> Play whole action of which takes place on clipper ship bound round the horn and winds up in Shanghai Brown's boarding house in Frisco—what year best (?)—look up data on Shanghai Brown, if any

He made notes for the play on 20 March, 14 May, and 6 and 13 October 1932; found the title, *The Calms of Capricorn,* on 8 March 1933; made further notes on 14 and 15 April and 7 May of that same year; and began to refer to the " '*Calms of Capricorn*' series"—apparently of four plays—on 4, 5, and 7 December 1934.

In this original conception of the Cycle each of the four sons of Simon and Sara Harford was to be the principal character of a particular play: Ethan, the sailor, would be the protagonist of *The Calms of Capricorn,* the first play; the second, "The Earth Is the Limit," was to be built around Wolfe, the gambler; the third, "Nothing Is Lost but Honor," would trace the rise and fall of the politician, Honey; and the fourth, "The Man on Iron Horseback," would follow the career of Jonathan Harford as a railroad and shipping magnate. But as O'Neill thought more and more about the four Harfords, he found himself inevitably involved with their parents and the action antecedent to *The Calms of Capricorn.* First Simon and Sara Harford, and then Sara's parents and Simon's mother took hold on his imagination and began to come alive for him. (He once wrote George Jean Nathan: "I never know how closely the characters, when they begin to live, will follow my plans for them.") On 27 January 1935, he had begun to make notes for the story of Simon and Sara as a new first play, making five plays in all.

On 3 February, when O'Neill found a new title for the Cycle, "A Touch of the Poet," he had definitely decided upon the "new first play of Sara—Harford—marriage—parents, etc." Between 6 and 24 February 1935, he wrote the scenario (getting a tentative title, "The Hair of the Dog," on 10 February 1935, and the final title, *A Touch of the Poet,* on 9 August 1937), but discovered that two plays would be necessary, the earlier dealing with Sara's parents and Sara and Simon's courtship, and the later concerning Simon's mother and Sara and Simon's married life together. He wrote the scenario for this second play of what was now to be a six-play Cycle (tentative title, "Oh, Sour-Apple Tree," 27 February; final title, *More Stately Mansions,* 22 March). Notes and the scenario for *The Calms of Capricorn*—the third play—occupied him from 27 April until 13 June 1935. By August of that same year the Cycle had again expanded—to seven plays—and it had a new title, "Twilight of Possessors Self-Dispossessed."

The seventh play, bringing the action down to 1932, was an old one, for which the initial idea, then titled tentatively "It Cannot Be Mad?," had occurred to O'Neill on 12 August 1927. He had then planned it as the second part of a trilogy, of which

Dynamo would be the first and *Days without End* the third. All three plays would deal with

> ... the general subject, more or less symbolically treated, of the death of the old God and the spiritual uneasiness and degeneration into which the sterile failure of Science and Materialism to give birth to a new God that can satisfy our primitive religious cravings has thrown us.

And they would eventually be published in a single volume as "Myths for the God-Forsaken." O'Neill worked on "It Cannot Be Mad?" intermittently over several years, changing the title to "On to Betelgeuse (Hercules)," and then to "The Life (Career) of Bessie Bowen (Bolan, Bowlan)," and apparently abandoning any idea of linking it to *Dynamo* and *Days without End*. He worked on an outline and notes, and actually wrote part of a first act in December 1934; but he complained in his *Work Diary* on 20 January 1935:

> this damned play won't come right—not big enough opportunity to interest me—should be part of something, not itself.

The next day, when some "grand new ideas" for the Cycle had occurred to him, he put "The Life of Bessie Bowen" temporarily out of his mind. When he at last returned to the play, at the end of August 1935, it had assumed its place as the final part of the seven-play Cycle.

Plans for the reconstruction of "The Life of Bessie Bowen" as "The Hair of the Dog" (the final title for this last play) were included in the rough outlines and notes that O'Neill made for all the Cycle plays, but he found that he could not carry any of them beyond this stage of preparation until the general themes for the series had been fully developed in the two first plays. (He tore up what he had written of the first act of "The Life of Bessie Bowen" on 21 February 1943.) Hence the impulse was backward in time. O'Neill later explained this to Elizabeth Shepley Sergeant in an interview on 24 August 1945:

... the difficulty, after [I] ... began to go backwards, was to find the starting point in all this—could never be sure of place where [I] ... ought to begin. Everything derived from everything else.

And so, having completed a first draft of *A Touch of the Poet*—the first of the Cycle plays to be written—on 18 March 1936, he wrote an initial draft of a new first play of an eight-play Cycle (tentative title, 7 September 1935, "Greed of the Meek"; final title—probably—9 August 1937, "And Give Me Death") between 19 March and 18 September, and a first draft of a still earlier play, the first of a nine-play Cycle (tentative title, "Give Me Death," 8 June 1936; final title, 9 August 1937, "Greed of the Meek"—the whole Cycle now to be called "Lament for Possessors Self-Dispossessed") between 11 August and 20 December 1937. Returning to these two plays in March 1938, O'Neill decided that it would be wisest to postpone rewriting them until he had finished all the others. He therefore wrote *More Stately Mansions* between 1 April and 8 September 1938, finished a second draft on 1 January and a third draft on 20 January 1939, and began the prologue for *The Calms of Capricorn* on 24 May. He finished a first draft of this preliminary scene on 3 June, but on 5 June decided it was "no good" and tore it up.

The need to go farther back in time finally proved stronger than the urge to write *The Calms of Capricorn* from its detailed scenario. On 20 October 1940, O'Neill went over the longhand scripts of the first two plays, analyzed them, and admitted to himself (in his *Work Diary*) that they were

> ... both as long as 'S[trange]. I[nterlude].'—too complicated—tried to get too much into them, too many interwoven themes & motives, psychological & spiritual.

Six months later he came reluctantly to the conclusion that the only possible solution for him was to expand the two plays into four. He commented in his *Work Diary* on 21 May 1941:

> have not told anyone yet of expansion of idea to 11 plays —seems too ridiculous—idea was first 5 plays, then 7,

then 8, then 9, now 11!—will never live to do it—but what price anything but a dream these days!

He subsequently prepared notes for this contemplated expansion, outlining the new first four plays and rewriting parts of *A Touch of the Poet* and *More Stately Mansions* in accordance with the new plan. To insure that the scripts as written would not influence him unduly in writing the first four plays of the eleven-play Cycle, he destroyed the longhand scripts for the first two plays of the nine-play Cycle in 1943. But his spirits were too depressed by world events and his health was too poor to make it possible for him to think of attempting then to write four new plays, and in desperation he determined to get *A Touch of the Poet* into something approaching final form. He succeeded in doing this mostly in 1942 and 1944. But the tremor in his hands often made it difficult if not impossible for him to hold a pencil, and his general health seemed to grow worse. In 1946, when he felt better, the O'Neills moved east to New York and all his energy went into rehearsals of *The Iceman Cometh* and *A Moon for the Misbegotten*.

Even as late as December 1948, O'Neill was still hoping to be able to work again. But early the next year he was finally obliged to admit that he would never write another play. Notes and drafts for Cycle plays were apparently torn up at Marblehead in 1951, but a substantial amount of manuscript material escaped destruction and was sent to Yale in that year. Included was the complete scenario for the fifth play of the nine-play Cycle, *The Calms of Capricorn*.

Although it is not even a first draft of the play as O'Neill would eventually have written it (notes for its reconstruction exist, made from time to time, especially in 1939 and 1941, while O'Neill was working on other plays), the scenario is sufficiently detailed and incorporates enough dialogue either directly or indirectly quoted so that the nucleus of the play O'Neill had in mind can be substantially recovered. Of course, O'Neill would not have permitted its publication and would have protested violently against the idea of its development into a play. He had warned Theresa Helburn and the Theatre Guild on 7 April 1936:

Don't begin to plan for the production of the Cycle, except in a very general way, until you receive finished plays from me to plan on. Don't expect first drafts. Mine are intolerably long and wordy—intentionally so, because I put everything in them, so as not to lose anything, and rely on a subsequent revision and rewriting, after a lapse of time with better perspective on them, to concentrate on the essential and eliminate the overweight. But to a person reading a first draft, that draft is the first impact of the play on them, and it is apt to be a very misleading impact indeed. My first drafts always bore me for long stretches, so I can hardly expect them to do less for other people. And being bored by a first draft would be a disheartening approach to this Cycle for the prospective producer.

The scenario is, at least in some aspects, both more and less satisfactory than a first draft. Its concision generally avoids the charges of excessive wordiness and the "too many interwoven themes & motives," which O'Neill acknowledged as faults of the first drafts of the first two plays of the nine-play Cycle. But, especially in scenes where the dialogue is only sketched, the speeches in their revelation of character and motive are the merest notes for what O'Neill would have made them. The scenario is, even so, of great documentary interest as the most nearly complete indication we have of O'Neill's plans for any of the unwritten Cycle plays.

Any further defense of the present publication is perhaps pointless. To some it will be a violation, pure and simple, of O'Neill's expressed wishes, and therefore indefensible. To others, it may be welcomed as giving additional invaluable details of the vast project to which America's foremost dramatist devoted most of his time, thought, and creative energies from 1934 to 1939—a period that should have been his most productive and mature. Fortunately, he succeeded in getting away from his obsession with the Cycle to write *The Iceman Cometh* (1939), *Long Day's Journey into Night* (1940), *Hughie* (1940), and *A Moon for the Misbegotten* (1941). And we do have the published *A Touch of the Poet* and *More Stately Mansions* as evidence of what the Cycle was to have been. Just as the latter play, in its incompletely revised state, comes far short of what O'Neill would doubtless have made it, so the scenario of *The Calms of Capricorn* is undeniably a great deal farther from what he had intended that play to be. But it does exist in manuscript, and its importance is so great that those responsible for its continued preservation believe that it should be made available for students of O'Neill's work. Its "development" into a more accessible form is designed merely to increase its readability, while adhering as closely as possible and with a minimum of elaboration to O'Neill's original text.

A NOTE ON THE
EDITORIAL METHOD

Passages in the play that are merely sketched by O'Neill in the scenario are marked by marginal lines; otherwise the words are substantially as he wrote them, with some minimal filling out, mostly of connectives. Where it is difficult to be certain of the speaker O'Neill intended or where reference of pronouns is unclear, choices obviously had to be made. As he wrote the scenario, O'Neill occasionally had second thoughts and, going back to earlier sections, noted changes to be made and wrote additional passages for insertion. These second thoughts have been incorporated in whole or in part, mostly without comment, where it seemed possible to do so; footnotes call attention to other changes that he contemplated making. (The reader should be warned that O'Neill in writing his plays often discarded such ideas without acting upon them.)

It was O'Neill's method to describe his characters as a part of his preliminary work on a play so that they would be firmly in his mind as he wrote. Such descriptions do not therefore, as a rule, appear in the scenario when characters are introduced. They have been taken for the most part from O'Neill's jottings and are inserted at the appropriate points in the play. O'Neill's miscellaneous notes for the revision of the scenario are the source for a few additional words of dialogue and one brief scene. Attention is called to these additions in footnotes.

O'Neill's scenario, transcribed following the play, is written in pencil on the rectos of seventeen quarto leaves in a leather-bound notebook containing, with notes for earlier plays, the scenarios of *A Touch of the Poet* (on twenty leaves) and *More Stately Mansions* (on twenty-eight leaves). An attempt has been made to present the text exactly as O'Neill wrote it, except that most misspellings (*e.g.,* "loosing" for "losing") have been silently corrected. An occasional slip of the pen has been explained (*e.g.,* "Goldie [*i.e.,* Leda]"). Doubtful readings have been questioned, thus: "[?]". Quotation marks and parentheses have been transcribed as they appear in the manuscript, whether or not they are both opened and closed. O'Neill's second thoughts appear either above the line, on the blank (facing) verso, or—in two instances—at the end of the scene. These additions have been incorporated in the transcript either as bracketed insertions or at the end of scenes as written. Words erased or cancelled by O'Neill have not been included.

The scenario was originally transcribed and much of the work on the play was done during the academic year 1968-69 when I was the recipient of a Guggenheim Fellowship for research on Eugene O'Neill's Cycle plays. Grateful acknowledgment is made to the John Simon Guggenheim Memorial Foundation for its support.

D. G.

New Haven, Connecticut
September 1981

THE PLAY

Scenes

Characters

SIMON HARFORD
SARA HARFORD, *his wife*
ETHAN HARFORD, *first mate, clipper ship* Dream of the West
WOLFE HARFORD, *clerk in a bank*
JONATHAN HARFORD, *clerk in a railroad office*
HONEY HARFORD, *tin peddler*
CAPTAIN ENOCH PAYNE, *captain of the ship*
THEODORE WARREN, *owner of the ship*
ELIZABETH WARREN, *his daughter*
BEN GRABER, *a banker*
LEDA CADE, *his companion*
THOMAS HULL, *former first mate of the ship*
JACKSON, *Ethan Harford's successor as first mate*
REVEREND SAMUEL DICKEY, *a minister*
NANCY DRUMMOND (MRS. ENOCH PAYNE), *wife of the Captain*
CATO, *a freed slave who works for the Harfords*
HELMSMAN
STEWARD
THIRD MATE
CREW
GOLD-SEEKERS

4

ACT ONE, SCENE ONE

Scene *The potato field on Sara Harford's farm. It is the spring of 1857, a fine morning.*

CATO, *a middle-aged Negro, a freed slave, is discovered. He is lazily making motions of work with a hoe, singing mournfully, grumbling aloud to himself.*

CATO

Freedom! I've had about all I want of it. Just the same old work, no freedom from that. Sure I earn a few dollars each month but I spend it all on whiskey and gambling and I'm broke the next day, so what good is it? I wish I was back in Georgia. What I'd give for some corn pone and chitlins! That was the life. The sun shone good and warm all day—not cloudy and miserable like here. And the folks who owned me were real quality, not trash like these Harfords. Master Simon they say was quality but he certainly isn't now. Of the children only Master Wolfe is my idea of a gentleman. As old Master used to say, the Irish trash coming in are ruining the country. But Miss' Harford is a fine woman in spite of that—only she expects me to work too hard, do ten men's work.

He sees her coming.

Here she comes, I'd better get to work. Oh, why did I ever let those fools persuade me to run off with them up north. And when they finally caught us in Massachusetts, why did Master Simon have to interfere and buy my freedom. He's the most interfering man.

He chuckles.

Old Master sure skinned him on the deal, got a thousand dollars for me, while in Georgia I'd have been dear at five hundred. Master Simon sure did know a fine buck when he saw one!

5

SARA *comes in, amused and exasperated. She is 47. There is a curious blending in her appearance of what are commonly considered to be aristocratic and peasant characteristics. She has a fine thoughtful forehead. Her deep-blue eyes are not only beautiful but intelligent. Her nose is straight and finely modeled. She has small ears set close to her head, a well-shaped head on a slender neck. Her mouth, on the other hand, has a touch of coarse sensuality about its thick, tight lips, and her jaw is a little too long and heavy for the rest of her face, with a quality of masculine obstinacy and determination about it. She wears a cheap calico work dress. She has thick ankles, large feet, and big hands, broad and strong, with thick, stubby fingers. Her fair complexion is tanned and her fine figure is still strong, firm, and healthy. There is a look of resigned sadness in her eyes and there are streaks of white in her black hair. Her voice is low and musical. She has rid her speech of brogue, except in moments of extreme emotion.*

SARA

Give me that hoe.

CATO

Resists, scandalized.

Why Miss' Harford, just supposing any of the white folks should see you.

He begins to work frantically.

I'll kill myself working rather than have you do such a thing. I don't want people saying I belong to a family whose Missus works in the fields like a hand.

He looks toward the farm.

What did I tell you? Here come some white folks calling. They see you here and they're coming up. Supposing I'd let you take the hoe?

SARA

It's Captain Payne and his wife. They know I've worked in the fields and never thought less of me.

CATO

They can't be quality, then. And you ain't worked since I came. Massa Harford he told me to see you didn't and I've done it.

CAPTAIN PAYNE and NANCY come in and exchange greetings.

He is in his 60s. His hair is white, he is of average height, his figure solid and imposing. He is dressed in the blue uniform of a ship's captain and gives an impression of conservatism, of being a man who would take no chances with the safety of his ship, its passengers, and its freight.

His wife, NANCY, is 38, still pretty, with a good figure. She has brown hair, with big brown eyes. She is shy, bashful, reserved, gentle. Her deep respect for her husband is apparent as is his love for her.

Lots more weeds down yonder. Excuse me.
He runs off.

SARA

Well this is a surprise. I didn't expect the ship in so soon.

PAYNE

We made a fine passage. Good winds from the Line up. Sensible sailing, not cracking on sail like those maniacs who'd ruin a good ship to get their names in the papers. I suppose I'm an old-fashioned sea dog. I love my ship.
He laughs, but with resentment.
Your son Ethan would tell you what an old fogey he thinks me. He has a craze for speed—to make a record even if you wreck the ship.

SARA

How is Ethan?

PAYNE

Fine.

SARA

Is he coming home to visit? I hoped he would, I wrote him his father had been ill. He didn't come to see us his last two trips, wrote that he would have too much work on board.

PAYNE

Smiles.

Well, that's hardly true, but Ethan is young; you mustn't mind. I suppose the real reason is that he has some girl in New York.

NANCY

Oh, no, I'm sure it's not that.

SARA

Looks at her.

Of course not. Any sign in New York of better times on the way?

PAYNE

No, it takes a good while to recover from a Panic. Well, that reminds me that I must drive on to make some calls—ship's business. I'll leave Nancy here with you and will call for her on my way back.

He goes.

SARA

Slyly pumping.

Well, Nancy, aren't you getting tired of life on the ship? I couldn't stand it, myself. I'm afraid of the sea. I still remember the crossing from Ireland with my parents, even though I was only a young girl, and how seasick I was then.

NANCY

No. The ship has become like home for me now. You know the reason I went—when our child died five years ago. The sea wipes out memory.

SARA

I suppose so. Tell me, Nancy, how is Ethan getting along?

NANCY

Embarrassed, then blurts out.

I wanted to speak about him. I think you ought to persuade him to change to another ship. He needs a change, his chance. I have studied Ethan. Of course, I don't pretend to understand him. He never confides, or hardly ever talks, but I am sure he feels thwarted, no chance to get on. There's a queer struggle always going on underneath between him and my husband. Ethan is so proud, so fierce; he was born to command. Captain Payne is an old friend of the ship's owner and, in spite of his age, is very healthy and so will never retire. Also the first mate has always sailed with him, and there's no chance for Ethan there.

SARA

Looks at her.

Then you think I ought to try and get him to go on some other ship?

NANCY

Yes, I think that would be best.

SARA

Well, there's only one way I ever discovered to get Ethan to do what you want and that's to advise him to do what you don't want and he'll be sure to act the opposite.

NANCY

Yes, he has a fierce pride in preserving his independence, in not letting anyone or anything get any hold on him, I feel that. That's why he hates the sea, because he loves it. But you must think it funny to have me discussing him so intimately. Why, really, I hardly know him. He's so reserved, so silent—and so entirely different from other men, you feel—so sensitive under his hard reserve, and so isolated and lonely in his freedom.

SARA

Yes, he's a touch of the poet in him, God pity him, like his father.

9

NANCY

Oh, but it's wonderful to have that touch of the poet in you, don't you think? Yes, Ethan is a poet, I've felt that.

SARA

Well, I'll do my best to get him out of your ship. I agree with you now that would be best.

NANCY

Frightened, reverses herself.

Ah, but don't take my word for it. I really shouldn't have spoken. I may be quite wrong. And, of course, Captain Payne would hate losing such a fine officer. He's really fond of Ethan underneath and I'm sure he'd be very angry if he knew I had spoken to you; so you must use your own judgment.

SARA

I will.

NANCY

Changes subject.

How is your husband?

SARA

Oh, never better. He's almost recovered from his illness. He has a new interest in life since he's been going with Honey on the tin wagon.

NANCY

Then he isn't working on his book?

SARA

Laughs.

No. He's taking a vacation from that. He'll never finish it, I'm thinking. He's all the time finding more he wants to put in it. It'll be in fifty volumes if he ever does finish it. But it keeps him occupied and not trying to help me on the farm. He was never cut out for a farmer.

She sees a rig drawing up to the house.

Why, it's Ethan!

She waves at him. Nancy is in an embarrassed flurry to get away but doesn't know how to manage it. ETHAN *comes in.*

10

He is 28. He is of medium height, but gives the impression of being taller, with a powerful, muscular body, full of intense, nervous vitality. He has straight light brown hair, a visionary's intense blue eyes set in a square, handsome, hawk-nosed face.

ETHAN

Mother!

SARA

Son! It's good to see you.

ETHAN

With formal polite indifference.

How do you do, Mrs. Payne.

NANCY

Hello, Ethan. I know you and your mother want to be alone. I'll meet Captain Payne on the road. I want to walk.

She goes.

SARA

Testing Ethan.

How pretty Nancy is!

ETHAN

Indifferently.

Is she? I suppose she is. I've never noticed. Just the wife of that old fool to me.

SARA

He was here a while ago. He was saying the reason you hadn't come home your last two voyages was you'd probably some girl you were after in New York.

ETHAN

He would think that.

SARA

It isn't true, then? It would be only natural.

ETHAN

No, it isn't true. I have no interest in women.

Then, bluntly.

The reason I didn't come home, if you must know, is that I was ashamed of always turning up the same old second mate. But here I am. I wasn't coming this time either—but, somehow, I suddenly felt lonely and homesick—a bit sick of the sea and its disappointments. And your letter about Father's illness had made me anxious. You wrote at such great length and said so much without really saying anything. You're not a very skillful liar, Mother. I take after you in that. But you succeeded in making me very curious. Perhaps that's what you wanted. Well, now I'm here, tell me what's happened.

SARA

Well, you know how he has lived in books ever since we came out here, and in the writing of his own book, going to his shack by the sea every morning to work, and wanting to help me on the farm in the afternoons, only I'd never let him.

ETHAN

You were wrong—made him ashamed.

SARA

I couldn't see him do it. He's a gentleman. And besides I'd always a feeling he didn't want me to let him help.

ETHAN

And yet he did want, I know. What was the last title of his book?

SARA

"The Meaning of Life."

ETHAN

Ah! No wonder he can't finish it!

SARA

He's given it up. He's destroyed it. He came to me one day and told me it was all a fake. Most of the days he's gone to the shack he'd never written a line but just sat and dreamed and stared at the sea. He cried. He said he'd been just a sponging loafer and a faker. But he'd done with dreams and

12

a barren solitude. There was still time to live. And then he quoted Whitman's "Song of the Open Road." And then what do you think? He said he'd go out on the wagon with Honey tin-peddling, and since he's done that he's a changed man, and full of gossip and the news of the world and politics. But there's something forced about it as if he was driving himself.

ETHAN

Forward to belonging? I know. But we Harfords are aliens now. We can never belong. Father always wanted this and that, too, but you can't have both. You must give this for that. He should have gone and lived alone, turned his back on his family, or should never have married. He has always remained a child, first tied to his mother's apron strings, then to yours.

SARA

Half indignantly, half comically.

Why the idea! That's nonsense! Still it has been a great sorrow to me, his going. I thought if we lived here simple on the land as he'd always said he wanted, he'd be happy at last.

ETHAN

You thought he knew what he wanted. But we Harfords don't. We only pursue a mysterious great need behind all wants, of which the wants are delusive shadows.

SARA

You sound unhappy.

ETHAN

I? No—only suffering from blind-alley sickness. I've been static too long. But if the wall doesn't move out of my way soon, I'll find some way to move it.

He forces a smile.

In plain words, I've been second officer too long, I'm getting nowhere.

SARA

Then why not change ship?

13

ETHAN

No, I can't explain the feeling I have—it must be this ship and no other. It is this because of my fate. It is the test, the particular challenge of the sea to me. I feel if I were to exchange and become captain in a day, it would be failure and cowardice—and how the sea would laugh in derision! To me the sea meant freedom from all land values, but I find myself still enslaved by them, always obeying orders. And I feel a love for the sea and hate it for that very reason. I want to break away, to experience all the freedom of the spirit. I'd like to go on to the conquest of high mountains, to tear their gold from them as a gesture of conquest.

SARA

Interested materialistically.

What about California? Jonathan wants to go. Why haven't you left the ship and gone to the mines?

ETHAN

At first scornful and insulted, then laughs.

I can't leave the sea unless I've conquered it first. I must leave it freed by my own choice as commander, not beaten by it and having to give it up.

SARA

Well, from being captain you could go on to partnership, then ownership and freedom.

ETHAN

Mother, possessions! Your freedom on this earth, this field, is that it belongs to you, but to me to be earthbound by possessions is slavery. What can it profit a man if he own the world and pay his soul for it? But I can see that for a woman the reverse is true, what could her soul profit her if she paid the earth for it?

SARA

I don't understand. What is it you want, Ethan?

ETHAN

I want nothing. It is what I need that I must have—must and will have—and will gladly pay the world for.

14

SARA

And what's that?

ETHAN

Victory over the sea—and so, freedom and rebirth.

SARA

I don't understand.

ETHAN

Not with your head, but with your heart you guess, for I know you love me, Mother.

SARA

I do.

ETHAN

And I speak to you in symbols which neither of us can think but which our hearts understand, because I love you, and because I love and hate the sea, which you can understand, being also a mother. For the sea is the mother of life, is a woman of all moods for all men, and all seductive and evil—devil mother or wife or mistress or daughter or waterfront drab. And it is as a sign and symbol of freedom to me that someday as captain of a ship I shall fight her storms and calms and fogs and crosscurrents and capricious airs and make a faster voyage around the Horn to the Golden Gate than ever man has made—as a last gesture of victory, now when the era of American triumph over the sea is dying from this money panic of the greedy earthbound. And if I smash the ship to pieces under me in the victory, well, one always pays for victory with one's temporal life that the soul may win freedom. I want this chance to accept the sea's challenge, that's all. If I win, I possess her and she cringes and I kick her away from me and turn my back forever. If I lose, I give myself to her as her conquest and she swallows and spews me out in death.

He looks at her troubled sad face and laughs.

But what has all this to do with freight rates and shipbuilding, you're wondering. And the answer to that is easy. Nothing, nothing at all.

He laughs.

Poor Mother. It must be a bitter blow to you to have such a mad offspring. Grandmother used to quote Byron to us—

SARA

Angrily, in brogue.

It's that old mad lunatic puts such thoughts in your head, trying to ruin you as she did your father.

ETHAN

Arrogantly.

No one can influence me, I am my own! No woman's!

SARA

Poor Nancy.

ETHAN

Eh? What?

SARA

Nothing. You say you love me—

ETHAN

And I do, don't doubt that. And I love Father, or perhaps I only pity him because I understand him. And, as for my brothers, I like Honey—and dislike Jonathan—and respect Wolfe because he respects nothing.

SARA

No, you don't even love yourself.

ETHAN

Ah, that's the point. I seek so to live that I may at the last come to a true self-respect that would be a reason for love.

He laughs.

Poor Mother, I say again. How I have unburdened myself to you. That's why I really came here, I see now, for I feel unloaded, freer, ready for a new voyage. But you look puzzled and sad.

He pats her hand.

Never mind. The brain is a latecomer. It knows nothing yet of life before it came. But the heart is old as life. It understands, eh, Mother?

SARA
Smiles and kisses him. In brogue.

It does, devil take it. It understands it's a hard fate for a woman to have been the daughter and wife and mother of men touched with the curse of the poet. For it's the moon you want and you hunt her in the skies of the broad day when the rest of us don't see her there at all.

She sees Honey and Simon coming out of the house. Alarmed.

I can't yawp at Honey.

She goes off. Ethan starts to follow her, then stops. She returns, accompanied by SIMON and HONEY, expostulating with Simon, bawling out Honey.

SIMON is 50, but looks much older. He is tall and loose-jointed, rather emaciated, still bearing the marks of having passed through a long and devouring fever. He has a long Yankee face, with Indian resemblances, swarthy, with a big, straight nose, a wide sensitive mouth, a fine forehead, with large ears. His brown hair is thinning. His light brown eyes, set wide apart, have a groping and bewildered stare. He speaks quietly, in a deep voice with a slight drawl.

HONEY is 24. He has a marked resemblance to his mother and is all peasant Irish. He is tall and heavily built, beginning to run a little to fat. He has curly black hair and inquisitive blue eyes, with a sparkle of sly, droll humor. His habitual expression is happy and good-natured.

HONEY
Greets Ethan.

But he insisted. I couldn't hold him down, and I thought a bit of sun and fresh air—

SIMON
Greets Ethan.

Yes, the sun will do me good.

17

SARA

Honey, you go help Cato.

He goes. She addresses Simon.

I feel you want to be alone with Ethan; I'll go to the house to see about the cooking.

She leaves.

From the end of the field comes Honey's voice singing, "The praties they grow small." *Simon and Ethan are silent, listening.*

SIMON

Do you know the last verse?

He recites the words and repeats those of the first verse. Then silence again.

You and I, Ethan, have always been strangers to each other, such strangers that I know there is a soul so identical in each that we have never felt the need to be anything but strangers.*

ETHAN

Yes, I have guessed that, Father.

SIMON

There is no father between us. Call me brother—or simply, man.

Strangely.

You will understand if I speak to you, after our lifelong silence, in words that would seem strange to those whose spirit has no ears. But I awoke just now from a dream of unity—a premonition and a prophecy, too, I think—

ETHAN

Catches this. Glances at him understandingly.

Yes, I think so. But let that be a secret between us.

---

* O'Neill's second thoughts (from the scenario):

Change this scene to Simon talking, Ethan humoring him with a sort of affectionate disdainful condescension—until father speaks of sea as she—

Or strange scene between them in which each talks about other but neither pays any attention to what other says until sea comes up

SIMON

The peace of that dream is still on me, and the intuition. In the dream the opposites at last blended and were one, and even now as the dream recedes, I am still in a place where the edges of the opposites still merge, and I can see and guess so much that is behind the senses. And I speak to the part of me which is three parts of you, and therefore is the dominant you, the you which is a fierce contempt for me and for yourself, a fierce pride and a lust for power and possession—but in the spirit, not the flesh. Can you hear me, man?

ETHAN

I hear you.

SIMON

I have only this to say. For you life is the sea. You think you will force your will on her and make her yours, and thereby dictate the terms by which she may possess you?

ETHAN

Right or wrong, it is the only way I can achieve meaning in my own eyes, expiate being myself, be able to forgive myself, be able to go on with pride. Right or wrong, it is my meaning.
Defiantly.
You do not think I can win? But I will win! Nothing shall stand in the way of my winning! Nothing! I will be as unscrupulous as the sea.

SIMON

I think you will lose, that if you win, you will have lost most of all. But I also know that your losing will be your final victory and release. But do not think I am presuming to advise you, or disapprove. On the contrary, you are doing the only thing that man, a lonely exile in a world of matter, can do—to choose his dream and then to follow that dream to the end.

Sara comes back, worried.

SARA

Simon, you must go in.

SIMON

Oh, no, I'll be all right.

19

ETHAN

I'm going to see Honey.

He goes off.

SIMON

There is something I feel I must say, Sara, trying to reach out to you over the gulf of our two solitudes. I feel a yearning love and regret for nature, love, the beauty of life—a hymn—a contempt for all reasons, explanations for living, all flights, alike for my own search for wisdom and your hunt for material possessions. What is life worth? The answer is so simple: life is worth one's life, one must pay for life with life. Oh to be able to give oneself to life and love and beauty—to belong—to let oneself be possessed in order to possess—to live and be free, to be freed by love. I love life, Sara, now, at the last, I love life and I love you. In this high noon, earth and spirit and you and I are one!

He hugs her to him.

SARA

Anxiously.

Simon, you are chilled, shivering!

SIMON

Smiles.

An old reaction of habit. I have always been chilled by the hot sun of high noon, I have always shuddered with cold in the arms of happiness, but no more. Now I shall find even the arms of night warm.

He quotes "Song of the Open Road."

SARA

Come to the house, by the fire.

SIMON

No, no. I am warmed in the warmth of your heart, Sara Beloved, warmed forevermore.

She clasps him fiercely to her.

Curtain

ACT ONE, SCENE TWO

Scene   *Sitting room of the farmhouse, two weeks later. Simon has died of pneumonia two days before. The four sons are discovered, waiting for the undertaker and hearse to come for the funeral. Sara is with the body in the next room.*

JONATHAN is 25. He resembles his father. He has a big head, is skinny and under medium height, with a long New England bony face. He is neat and respectable in his dress. He has light brown hair, sharp intelligent hazel eyes, and a big nose. He gives the impression of being older than his years, full of tense nervous vitality, but remarkably self-disciplined and sure of his own capabilities.

WOLFE is 27. He is tall and thin, handsome, distinguished, fastidious—a mixture of his father and his mother—with a pale aristocratic face. He suppresses all emotional reaction under a mask of smiling indifference. A man's man.

JONATHAN

It would be folly for Mother to cling to this farm. She needs a complete change to get over her terrible grief. I know a purchaser for the farm. Let's sell and all go to California. There's a great chance out there, in the mines. We are all stagnating here. [Besides, we owe it to Mother to make up to her, give her back the life she's given to Father and to us. Father was a bit crazy from Grandmother Harford.]*

HONEY

Father wasn't crazy. He was a poet and Mother loved him and so did I. But he's dead now and we must do everything we can for Mother, help her to forget.

* Bracketed words are from O'Neill's notes for the revision of the play.

21

JONATHAN

What do you think, Ethan?

ETHAN

Antagonistic and contemptuous.

I know nothing of your money-grubbing values and don't want to know.

They quarrel.

But the sea voyage might be good to help Mother forget, and when she gets to California she can decide. But can we get her to give up this land—her obsession? Only if we all urge her as one.

JONATHAN

Turns to Wolfe contemptuously.

And you, I suppose you don't care whether you stay or go?

WOLFE

With his quiet, enigmatic smile.

No. So I am perfectly willing to go.

JONATHAN

And you, Honey?

HONEY

Anywhere where there's gold to be got without working too hard for it, that's the land for me.

Then, conscience-stricken.

But it's no time to be talking and planning with Father lying dead in the next room, though he used to do a lot of talking himself to me on the wagon about going to California. But the way he talked, California was only a fairyland in his mind.

JONATHAN

It's too bad we didn't get closer to Father, to help him more, though he certainly wasn't much help to Mother.

HONEY

His written directions for the funeral service were queer. He meant something for us by them but what only he will ever know.

22

JONATHAN

Get Mother, Honey. She'll wear herself out in there. She has hardly spoken, except to him, since he died. If we could get her to talk, maybe she'd get it out of her system. We don't want her to collapse.

> *Honey goes out and brings* SARA *back with him.
> They hold a service—the undertaker is due soon
> —each has a part of a poem to read, then Honey
> a verse of a song to sing, and then as finale Sara
> opens an envelope and reads what Simon has
> written for her to read.*

SARA

"My Beloved: You have done your duty by me, given your life in love to protect, comfort, and save me, but now that I am dead, that life is over. A new life is opening up for you and you must not let my memory stand in your way, you must forget me and be free."

> *She reacts to this with reproachful, despairing
> tenderness.*

Forget you, Simon? It's little you know of love, God help you! By all that's good I swear to remain faithful to your memory and the beautiful memory of our whole life together. For it was a wonderful life, with great happiness as well as sorrow—

JONATHAN

Mother! Stop. Don't torture yourself.

HONEY

No, don't stop her, Jonathan. Go ahead, Mother, and say all that's in your heart. Of course your life together was wonderful.

SARA

Yes, he was a poet, a child, too good for this world. But I should have done more for him, should have understood him better, should never have let my greed take him into business. I should have done all the work and left him free for his high thoughts of beauty and search for the wisdom of life. I should never have let him return to his mother, for that brought his loneliness back to him. He had a lovely soul in him and if he'd

23

only given me that soul how I would have loved and protected it! But he wanted to and it wasn't in his power, it was a cross laid on him, a curse he couldn't shake off.

Fiercely.

And why am I complaining? Wasn't it a beautiful life I've lived, even the sorrow of it? How many women have known what I have known, the feel inside that your heart has borne the man you love into life, and in your heart he's grown and become a man and your lover and husband and yet always remained a child, and at the last his death is only a return behind the gates of birth to sleep at peace again forever in the love of your heart.

She rises to a pitch of passionate exultation.

Yes, I thank Almighty God for you, Simon, and for the beautiful dream of the poet's love, and the passion of a man's love, and the tender dependence of a child's love you brought to me. And it's the sweet life I've lived with you and I wouldn't change it if I had a choice of all the lives other women have ever lived in the world!

> *A knock sounds at the door. Jonathan goes out and returns.*

JONATHAN

It's the undertaker. He has only one man with him, so we'd better help.

SARA

Wait a minute, I want to say a final good-bye.

HONEY

We'll hold him in the hall till you give the word, Mother.

> *All four sons go out. Sara goes to the doorway, stops, suddenly feeling awed.*

SARA

How withdrawn he looks. I feel I'm intruding on his privacy. He was always such a gentleman, so modest, would never let me see him naked, and now he seems naked to me, so bare and lonely. What will he do now without me?

Then, sadly.

24

But he always was without me, even when he was most with me.

Then, desperately.

Simon! this once—only this once—give me all of you for the all of me!

Then sobbing.

Forgive me, I have no right to ask it. I'm always thinking of myself. Sure, I know you can't, and I'll be happy in your happiness, for don't I know you're happy now. For at last you're free, free even of me, and God bless and preserve you in that freedom!

She turns and stumbles blindly to the hall door.

Take him now and be quick about it.

She remains there, speaking as if thoughts were running through her mind without her volition.

Free of me—free of me—and you've set me free. I've a new life starting and I'll do as I please now and as I've always wanted and I've four strong sons to work with me and to help me to the wealth and power of this world and all I've dreamed.

A sound of hammering comes from the next room. In a frenzy of sorrowful, savage denunciation.

Arrah, are those the thoughts you're having now, you shameless creature! May God curse you for a greedy sow and no woman at all!

Then, pitifully.

Simon! You didn't hear, did you? And if you heard, sure it's well you must know it's not your love speaking at all!

Renewed hammering from the next room.

Curtain

ACT TWO, SCENE ONE

Scene *After-cabin of the clipper ship* Dream of the
West *at dock in New York, six weeks later.*
JONATHAN *and* HONEY *come out of their stateroom at right, Honey boyishly enthusiastic and
awed by the splendid accommodations.*

JONATHAN

It's all well enough for sail, but the sailing ships are dead.
Steamers will make this look like nothing.

THE REVEREND MR. DICKEY *comes out of his
room at right. He is 34. He is a typical Prot-
estant minister, rather shabbily dressed in con-
servatively somber habit, of average height and
build. A slightly unctuous expression is charac-
teristic of him. He wears glasses that give him
a somewhat myopic look.*

DICKEY
Unctuously.

How do you do. I am the Reverend Samuel Dickey.

HONEY

How do you do, sir. I am Honey Harford and this is my brother
Jonathan.

JONATHAN

How do you do.

DICKEY

My cabin mate is a Mr. Harford.

HONEY

Our brother.

The Reverend Mr. Dickey goes out. WOLFE
comes out of the same cabin.

Well, you didn't have very good luck with your roommate.

26

Wolfe smiles indifferently.

JONATHAN

I'm going out on the dock, to have a look at New York.

HONEY

Well, don't buy it.

JONATHAN

Come on.

HONEY

No, I'll wait for Mother. Nancy is showing her her cabin.

JONATHAN

How about you, Wolfe?

WOLFE

Is starting to play a game of solitaire.
Indifferently.

Oh, I guess not.

Jonathan goes out, contemptuously.
SARA *and* NANCY *come out of Nancy's cabin.*

SARA

The cabins are beautiful and there's so much room!

NANCY

Addressing Wolfe.

We put your mother right next to us so that I can look after her.

SARA

How long before the ship sails?

HONEY

Teases her.

You may well ask, for you were certainly in a stew to get us here hours before time!

SARA

I remember how your grandfather nearly missed the boat coming over from Ireland.

27

NANCY
Laughing.

You are quite right to avoid the last-minute crush, although in these hard times the ship is normally half empty. But this voyage, for some strange reason, the second-cabins forward and the steerage are full up with a company of gold-seekers, all from the same neighborhood in northern New York. It seems from what Captain Payne heard that their leader had news from his brother in California of a big new strike and he'd gotten a company together of poor neighbors. It will be like the first days. Poor things, I hope they have better luck than those others, that this wonderful new strike isn't just a fairy tale.

HONEY
Impressed.

Say, I'd better talk with them, get in on it.*

NANCY
To Wolfe.

Don't you ever stop playing that game?

WOLFE
With strange, pleasant but remote smile.

It keeps me from thinking, and hoping, and all the rest of it. It's pure art, without object except itself, no gain.

NANCY

But don't you ever play with someone?

WOLFE

No, that would be to involve myself in the outside game.

Sara sighs over him helplessly.

HONEY
Taunts him.

You're afraid of being beat.

* O'Neill's second thoughts (from the scenario):
Introduce scene Ethan & Sara (& Nancy?)—their congrats his promotion—Sara tells him sure he owes it to Nancy—he is formally thankful—but joking in comical seriousness, says he feels other woman in it, fate—father told me sea was woman—

WOLFE
Calmly.
No, except insofar as being beaten would imply that the competitive game was worth winning.

NANCY
Laughs.
You're a funny boy, Wolfe.

WOLFE
Yes, I agree. I know it will sound incredible but I am always watching myself from inside and laughing. But then I'm laughing at everyone else, too.

SARA
A bit exasperated.
Don't mind his nonsense. He needs a few good hard knocks to wake him from his dreaming and I'm hoping he'll get them in California, or maybe one or two starters on this voyage.
Then, smiling.
But he's a good boy, Nancy, and if his head's full of queer dreams, it's only the touch of the poet in him he gets from his father, God rest his soul.

NANCY
But surely you're enthusiastic about your brother Ethan's being appointed first mate at last.

WOLFE
Smiling, without looking up from cards.
I don't know. Should I be? I would have to be sure first that it is fortunate to get what one wants.

NANCY
Oh!

HONEY
Shrewdly.
Is it sure he's got it? We haven't started yet. Maybe the first mate will show up.

NANCY
Oh, no. His doctor told the Captain only this morning that his heart was in no condition, he must rest for one voyage at least,

29

and even a headstrong man like Mr. Hull is bound to heed that advice. I told the Captain at once he owed it to Ethan. He rather hesitated, you know he feels Ethan is young and reckless, but I said I'd talk to Ethan and make him behave, and besides, with his mother on board, he'd be bound to be on his best behavior; so the Captain gave in.

> *She laughs joyously.*

Oh, aren't you all glad? Poor Ethan, he's waited so long and had so many disappointments.

> *Sara glances at her queerly. Nancy grows confused.*

Oh, I suppose it's wrong of me to rejoice over Mr. Hull's illness but it's really not serious, I believe, and then I feel toward Ethan as you must feel—like a mother—and I know how much he wanted this promotion. He was so excited when he moved his things into Mr. Hull's stateroom—like a boy who's won a prize.

> *Then, again catching Sara's eye, she breaks off and changes the subject abruptly.*

But I haven't told you we're to have the owner, Mr. Warren, and his only daughter, Elizabeth—he's a widower, she's just eighteen.

SARA

> *Perks up.*

Ah, so the owner and his only daughter—

HONEY

> *Teases her.*

Making a match for one of us already?

> *Sara, guilty, but laughs it off.*

Which is it? It isn't me for you wouldn't have the heart to part with me, you need me to look after you.

SARA

Listen to him!

HONEY

It can't be Wolfe here for you know very well he wouldn't look at the Queen of Sheba herself, much less marry her, for that would involve him in the game, as he calls it, and make him start living. Isn't that right, Gentleman?

WOLFE
Smiles.
Exactly. I hereby make over my share in women to you, Honey.

HONEY
But maybe I'll hold you to that promise some day. And it won't be Jonathan, will it, Mother? He's too busy scheming how he'll grab the world away from whoever owns it to bother —unless the girl's father owned the world and he'd see marrying her as a shortcut. But this girl's father only owns ships, so— It must be Ethan then, Mother. He's a sailor and she'd be in his line.

NANCY
Interposes indignantly.
Nothing of the sort. I've met her. She's spoiled, proud, cold as ice—and delicate. Her health's the excuse for the voyage, although I think that's only a pose, which she thinks makes her interesting. Oh no, she's not the wife for Ethan at all. He needs someone healthy and warm and loving, able to take care of him.
A STEWARD *comes in carrying bags.*
Ssshh—must be them now.

CAPTAIN PAYNE *enters with* WARREN *and* ELIZA-BETH, *makes introductions.*

Payne and Nancy accompany the Warrens to their cabin.

WARREN *is 48. He is a tall, full-chested man, with a fine-looking Roman face, his clothes expensively conservative. He has the look of success, of financial prosperity, stamped on him from long habit.*

ELIZABETH *is 18. She is tall, dark, slender, with a boyish figure, a wiry body, full of intense ner-*

31

vous energy beneath a coldly beautiful, calm, disciplined exterior. She gives the impression of being aloof and something of a snob.

SARA

She does look like a proud piece; but Ethan is proud, too, and she's beautiful.

Honey laughs. PAYNE *comes back.*

When do we sail, Captain?

PAYNE

Soon now. Two other cabin passengers are due, we won't wait for them.

SARA

Who are they?

PAYNE

A man and wife. By the way, congratulations on Ethan's promotion. I must confess that it was Nancy's doing.

He turns back to the cabin as ELIZABETH, NANCY, *and* WARREN *come out.*

SARA

He's a decent, pleasant old man—but a blind old fool all the same.

HONEY

What do you mean, Mother?

SARA

Nothing.

As the others rejoin them, A STEWARD *comes in with bags, followed by* GRABER *and* LEDA.

GRABER *is 53, but looks older. One senses at once that he is a broken man inside. There is a furtiveness about him, as if he were in constant fear of being caught. A rather gross figure, with a slightly unkempt air about it, rather seedy. He is drunk.*

32

LEDA *is 25. She has a beautiful, opulent femi-*
nine figure, a trifle gross, replete with a nerveless
animal health, exuberance, and self-security. She
has a big-featured, handsome, frankly sensual
face. She is all emotion, intuitive, female instinct;
is capable of passionate bursts of anger, hatred,
or love, and of a measureless lethargic calm. Her
appearance strikes everyone into stunned silence.

GRABER
Follows the steward blindly.

Come on, m'dear.
He goes into their cabin.
Leda stands looking from one to another with a
mocking, amused defiance.

LEDA

Good morning!

PAYNE
Flustered, feels called upon to make introduc-
tions.

Mrs. Graber, isn't it?
He introduces her to the women. She gives each
a searching glance.

LEDA
To Sara, smiling.

I *am* glad to meet you. I'm sure we'll understand each other.
To Nancy.

Yes, I think I know you.
To Elizabeth, who snubs her, sharply.

You are not fooling me. I know you, too—and what you want
from me.

ELIZABETH

I?
Warren starts to splutter.

LEDA
To the Captain.

You needn't bother introducing the gentlemen, Captain. I have
met them all before.

She laughs.

You needn't look so embarrassed. I mean others so like you it makes no difference.

Then, to Ethan.

Except you. No, I've never met you before—but I will now, of course.

ETHAN
Smiles, pleasantly amused.

I think not.

LEDA
Smiles.

You do? Well, we'll see.

GRABER
Sticking his head out of the stateroom.

Leda, aren't you coming?

LEDA

I'll be right there, Ben.

She bows.

I'll have the pleasure of seeing you all later.

She goes in.

WARREN
Sputters.

Captain Payne, how could you introduce that woman to my daughter?

ELIZABETH
Coldly, commandingly.

Never mind, Father. The lady made no impression on me whatsoever.

Then forces a laugh.

But I admire her impudence. What I want from her indeed!

She gives a little shudder of disgust.

But I do feel the air will be a bit purer out on deck. Such rank beastly perfume! Are you coming, Father?

She goes out.

WARREN
Indignantly, to the Captain.

Graber! Did you hear? An actress—or maybe even out of a
house—before she married. If I had known she was to be a
fellow passenger, I'd have had the office tell her we were full.
Well, we'll have to make the best of it. I've no doubt she'll
keep to herself.

ETHAN *enters.*

ETHAN
Captain, the tug is standing by.

Much commotion outside and HULL *enters. He
is in his late 50s, a typical seaman, with a lined
weather-beaten face and a constant sour expression.*

HULL
Of course I'm able to make the trip. There's nothing wrong
with my heart.

PAYNE
Secretly relieved.

Well, all right. Sorry, Ethan
To Warren, on side.
Don't you think this is best?

WARREN
Well, I suppose so. I've often thought you could make a
speedier voyage, but of course the safety of the ship and the
passengers must be considered, and repair bills, and Hull's
long service with you.

HULL
Caustically, to Ethan.

Afraid I'll have to trouble you to move your gear back to your
own cabin.

Ethan seems to be about to explode.

SARA
Ethan!

ETHAN
Turns to Hull.
Very good, sir—and I congratulate you on your recovery.

PAYNE
Heartily approves.
That's a fine lad. And now, make ready to sail.

> *Ethan and Hull go out and Payne and Warren follow.* LEDA *has come in and witnessed the interview.*
>
> GRABER *comes out.*

SARA
What a disappointment for Ethan!

NANCY
Furious.
Hull did it just in spite.
> *She bursts into tears.*

LEDA
Pats her on the back.
Never mind. I don't like that Hull, I know his kind, they never want to admit they're too old. They'd like to murder youth. But perhaps he'll fall overboard or we can give him a push.

> *Nancy is horrified. Honey laughs.*

GRABER
Greets Wolfe.
Well, I'm glad to see there's someone on board I can have a game with.

> *In the background the company of gold-seekers begin to sing as the ship moves from the wharf.*

HONEY
Come on, Mother. I want to join in.

SARA
No, I think I'll stay here.

HONEY

Come on, Wolfe.

They go off.

GRABER

Nervous, haunted now.

Come on, Leda. Let's see the last of New York—and maybe
I'm not glad to see the last of it!

LEDA

Warns him.

Careful, Ben! No, I'll stay here. You go.

He leaves. She addresses Nancy.

You know you shouldn't show your feelings so openly. Of
course, the old man would never see, but others have sharper
eyes and might tell him.

NANCY

Confused and horrified.

I don't know what you mean.

LEDA

Oh, yes, you do. And you needn't be afraid with me. I'm an
absolutely impure woman, you see. It means nothing to me
what anyone does or how or why they do it.

NANCY

Stammers.

Why—I—

ETHAN enters. Nancy, hysterically to him.

Oh, Ethan, I'm so sorry.

Ethan is repelled.

LEDA

To Nancy.

Introduce me.

NANCY

This is Mrs. Graber, Ethan.

LEDA

Hard luck.

ETHAN

Stares at her.

Yes, it is.

LEDA

But luck changes.

ETHAN

When?

LEDA

Sometimes when you least expect it. And you—I think you've about reached the point where you make it change.

> HULL *comes down the companionway.*
> *He sneers at Ethan.*

HULL

Well, well, here you are, entertaining ladies when you ought to be on deck.

ETHAN

Tries to be patient.

I saw a moment when I thought I could get my stuff out of your cabin.

HULL

Gloats.

You thought I was finished this time, thought you'd sneak sail on her, and maybe Captain would take sick or, better still, die.

NANCY

Angrily.

How dare you! I'll report you to the Captain.

HULL

Sneers.

Maybe I'll have a report to make to him, too, Missus. I'm older than him but not as blind.

> *Then to Ethan, insultingly.*

Get out of here where you belong!

> *Ethan turns, meets Leda's eyes.*

LEDA
With contempt.

Is this the wonderful discipline on ship I've heard about, that
you stand for every insult and are afraid to hit back?

> *Ethan whirls, smashes Hull on the jaw. Hull
> falls, hits his head on the stairs, lies still. Nancy
> stifles a scream. Ethan looks down. Leda kneels,
> and examines Hull.*

LEDA
Simply.

Dead.

ETHAN

Dead?

LEDA

Yes, that's what you really meant, isn't it?

NANCY

No! You didn't mean to kill him, did you, Ethan?

LEDA
To Ethan.

You go out on deck. Hurry!
> *He goes. Then, to Nancy.*

And now you and I will do a little lying. He slipped coming
down. We were here. We saw him. He hit his head. That's all.
You hear me?

NANCY
Staring down at the body, with a shudder.

Yes.

LEDA

What's the matter? You're glad he's dead, aren't you?

NANCY

No, no, how can you?

LEDA

Don't be a hypocrite!

NANCY

Yes, yes, I am glad. I am. It's true. Why shouldn't I say it?

LEDA

Good! Now you're talking like a real woman. And now you're looking at this dead old man and thinking of another old man and that if only he were—

NANCY

No, no. You're horrible. Oh, I hate you. You're evil. Stop putting thoughts in my head. Go away—or, I can't help it, I'll scream!

> *She shrieks and Leda screams with horror with her. Then Leda grabs her as she is about to faint.*

LEDA

That's good. That's what I wanted you to do—to scream with horror when we found out he was dead. Ssshh! They're coming. Remember what we must tell them now.

> *Nancy bursts into violent sobbing.*

Curtain

ACT TWO, SCENE TWO

Scene   *The same, a few minutes later. The* CAPTAIN *is just straightening up from examining the first mate's body.* WARREN *stands beside him.*

WARREN

Well?

PAYNE

Nothing to do. He's gone.

NANCY
Hysterically.

He just slipped coming down the companionway and fell. Sara and Leda saw it, didn't you?

PAYNE
Pats her on the arm.

I know. You've told us before.
To Warren.

I suppose in his condition, heart weak—dizzy spell and fell.

WARREN

Yes, a terrible accident.
Forces laugh.

Not a very favorable omen to start the voyage, eh? I'm glad I'm not superstitious.

Elizabeth's voice calls down imperiously from the door of the companionway, "Father! I want to know what has happened! Tell this man to let me come down!" *Warren signals to the sailor above guarding the entrance.*

No, no!

SAILOR'S VOICE

Sorry, Miss. My orders.

41

WARREN

I'm coming right up, Elizabeth—coming right up.

To Captain.

I suppose you'll send his body back by the tug?

PAYNE

Yes.

WARREN

I'll keep my daughter out of the way. She mustn't see death—never has—a terrible shock to one so delicate and high-strung. I'll go to her.

He passes LEDA *by the companionway.*

LEDA

With drawling mockery.

It might do her good. There's nothing like the sight of death—to wake people up and start them living.

WARREN

Stops and stares at her fascinatedly.

Yes. One sees there is so little time left, and one has missed so much—and one is growing old.

She gives a little throaty laugh. He snaps out of the mood she has cast on him; frigidly.

I beg your pardon, I don't know what you're talking about. Will you kindly let me pass?

LEDA

Of course—if you want to.

He goes up the companionway.

PAYNE

Steward, will you ask Mr. Harford to come here please.

Steward goes.

NANCY

Misunderstanding, breaks out hysterically.

Why do you want him? What has he to do with it? He wasn't here.

Payne looks at her in surprise.

42

SARA

Breaks in hastily.

The Captain will be wanting to tell him he's first mate now again and give him his orders.

PAYNE

Still stares at his wife, in the back of his head an aroused wonder which is the germ of suspicion; a bit sharply.

Naturally. What else?

NANCY

Flustered.

Of course. How silly of me! I—

Door at left, rear, from main deck opens and closes; it is not Ethan but WOLFE. *He stands there for a moment. The Captain, after a glance at him, looks with bowed head and growing grief at the mate's body. Wolfe approaches, looks down at the body with cool indifference. Leda watches him interestedly. He shrugs his shoulders, turns away, goes to the table, mechanically takes the cards out from a drawer, and begins his solitaire. Leda comes and stands behind him.*

PAYNE

A sob shakes his shoulders. He mutters.

Poor Tom—old friend—forty-five years we've sailed the seven seas together—and now—

NANCY

Breaks out hysterically.

Don't, Enoch! I can't bear it!

PAYNE

Startled out of his grief, sees Wolfe playing, blazes into anger.

Put away those cards, sir! Damn you, have you no respect for the dead?

SARA
Joins in.
Yes, Wolfe. Don't be so heartless.

WOLFE
Gathers the cards together coolly.
Sorry, Captain. You think he cares? It seemed to me the dead are so entirely indifferent to our little games.

LEDA
Laughs, pats him on the cheek.
I like you.

PAYNE
Bursts out.
It is no question, sir, of what—

ETHAN *has come in. He addresses the Captain quietly.*

ETHAN
You wanted me, sir?

Payne turns to him.

NANCY
Bursts out.
Mr. Hull slipped coming down the companionway and fell.

PAYNE
Yes, that's apparently what happened.

ETHAN
Looks down at the body calmly.
He's dead?

PAYNE
Yes.
Then angrily.
Damn it, you say that as if you were talking of a dead dog! And you've sailed with him for eight years. Have you no feelings?

44

ETHAN

Calmly.

I have no hypocrisy, sir, if that's what you mean. There was never anything but enmity between him and me. I cannot pretend a grief I do not feel.

NANCY

Bursts into sobs.

Oh, Ethan, how can you be so unfeeling—so cruel to me—?
Wildly.
I mean, to him, to him!

SARA

Warningly.

Ssshh! Ssshh!

ETHAN

Gives her a glance of cold scorn. Turns to Captain.

I am to be first mate now?

PAYNE

With resentful anger.

Yes, Mister—for this voyage. I make no promises beyond that. It all depends—and I tell you frankly I wouldn't appoint you now if I had any choice—I—
Angrily.
Go take your duties, Mister—and I want to warn you—no trickery on your watch—no sneaking sail on her when I'm asleep, for I'll wake. Obey my orders strictly, Mister, or, by God, I'll put you for'ard among the crew!

ETHAN

Unruffledly.

Very good, sir.

Turns and starts up companionway.

PAYNE

Wait—you seem to profit by misfortune. The second mate fractured his skull—now the first mate. I suppose you're hoping I'll fall too, and break my head, and then you'll have your

45

You'll command her, wrack her to pieces to break
d.

NANCY

*Runs, throws her arm around his neck, hysteri-
cally.*

No! Don't say such things! Ethan doesn't want you dead—why
it's like saying I want you dead!

*She kisses him, sobbing. He is immediately
ashamed of himself.*

PAYNE

Holds out his hand to Ethan.

I'm sorry, my boy, I'm sorry, Ethan. I'm upset. Forget it.

ETHAN

Shakes his hand.

Of course, sir. If you don't want me any further, I'd better—

PAYNE

Yes, take over, Mister.

Ethan goes. Payne breaks from Nancy.

I've got to go on deck. Will you take her to her cabin, Mrs.
Harford?

*He goes up companion. Sara starts with Nancy
toward the cabin.*

LEDA

Pats Nancy on the back.

Not so bad for a beginner, but you'll have to do better—before
this voyage is over.

NANCY

*Looks up, stares fascinatedly into her eyes,
bursts out in an excited whisper.*

Yes, I made him believe, didn't I? He'll never guess, will he?
He'll never guess.

Then horrified at herself, to Sara.

Oh, take me away. Make her go away!

Hides her face on Sara's bosom.

46

SARA
Stares at Leda.

I'm thinking you're a strange, hard woman, but not half as hard as you'd like to make out.

LEDA
Laughs.

You think so? Maybe so. Maybe not. What's the difference?

SARA
Crosses herself.

I'm afraid it's an unlucky voyage.

LEDA

What is bad luck for one makes good luck for another, and it all winds up even in the end.

> *Sara leads Nancy into the cabin. Wolfe has taken out his cards and begun to play again. Leda turns to him.*

WOLFE
Quietly.

I feel something in the air. What is it? Did Ethan murder our friend there?

LEDA

Don't ask questions. You don't really care whether he did or not, do you?

WOLFE

No—except I'm interested in seeing Ethan get what he thinks he wants in order to watch him throw it away.

LEDA

And what do you want, Wolfe?

WOLFE

Nothing.

LEDA

Not even me?

WOLFE

Not even you.

LEDA

I'll make you want me before we're through. Want to bet?

WOLFE

I never bet, I only play for nothing.

LEDA

Afraid you'd lose?

WOLFE

Stung.

I'm not afraid of anything! I'll take any bet you like. But I
have nothing.

LEDA

You have yourself.

WOLFE

That is the greatest and commonest illusion.

LEDA

Eh?

WOLFE

But if you accept it, all right. I bet myself.

LEDA

Against myself.

WOLFE

Done!

LEDA

Done.

> HONEY *and* GRABER *enter, tipsy, singing* "Sacra-
> mento."

GRABER

Very drunk.

Those gold-seekers for'ard are good fellows but fools.

> *Sees the dead mate, thinks him drunk.*

An officer of the ship in such condition!

LEDA
Shocked into indignation, bawls him out.

You fool! The man's dead.

Graber immediately terrified, rushes to her, clings to her for protection. She soothes him contemptuously. Honey awed, crosses himself. Graber whispers in Leda's ear.

Shut up that superstitious junk. This has nothing to do with you. God, to think I'd ever get tied up to a man with a conscience!

WOLFE
Quietly.

That's bad singing, but the dead are the only ones it can't disturb, I should think.

Leda takes this as a reproach, becomes flip again.

THE REVEREND MR. DICKEY *enters.* *

DICKEY

The Captain told me to come here.

LEDA
Breaks in mockingly.

Yes, something in your line. Show us your best stuff, take the curse off this voyage. I'll join in the hymns. You may not believe it but I had the strictest kind of religious bringing up. I owe all my success to that—

He stands, gaping at her in shocked horror.

You don't believe me? Listen!

She sings "Fields of Eden." Graber and Honey laugh and applaud. Dickey turns his back on them, kneels by the corpse, and begins to pray.

Curtain

---

* O'Neill's second thoughts (from the scenario):
  Ship starts from dock just after Dickey's entrance?

ACT THREE, SCENE ONE

Scene   *The clipper becalmed in the south Atlantic in late November, evening, looking astern from the main deck at the break of the poop, interior of Ethan's cabin at right, center, front, and interior of after-cabin revealed. In Ethan's cabin, he is discovered lying asleep on bunk, almost fully dressed, turning restlessly in his sleep. On poop deck above, grouped to right and left of the mast, are, seated on deck chairs, from right to left,* NANCY, SARA, JONATHAN *(to the right of the mast),* WARREN, ELIZABETH, *and* DICKEY.

NANCY

I've never seen a calm here before at this time of year. I'm afraid it has ruined our chances of tying the *Flying Cloud*'s record to the Tropic of Capricorn.

WARREN

Well, after all, the record passage to the Line was sheer luck, there never was such a favoring wind. The Captain was forced into a record, he even seemed to resent it or be afraid of it. But from the Line to the Tropic if he'd cracked on we'd have crossed the Tropic days ahead of the *Flying Cloud* and we could have afforded this calm. When Ethan set on more sail in his watch without orders and had that row with the Captain about it, I thought the Captain was right at the time, but now, I don't know. I'm not one to approve recklessly going after the record for the record's sake, but in these slack shipping times when the record is thrust on one, it's one's duty to get that advantage, to follow one's luck.

JONATHAN
Impatiently.
There is no luck. One makes luck with one's will.

50

Then, flatteringly.
I'm sure that's what you've done in your success, sir.

Warren is pleased.

NANCY
As if coming out of a dream.
You think one must make one's opportunities for—for happiness? But that makes life so terrible.

JONATHAN
No, that's all that makes life worth living.

DICKEY
That's not a very Christian sentiment. One must bow to the will of God—but, of course, if you mean that one must take every opportunity to seek grace, to save one's own soul—

JONATHAN
Dryly.
I know nothing of the soul—what shall it profit—?

DICKEY
Oh, come now. That's blasphemy.

ELIZABETH
I don't think it is. I believe it's what I want in this life.

Jonathan is pleased. Nancy strangely moved.

JONATHAN
Turns to Nancy.
And happiness is beside my point. One sees one's goal, fixes on it, then devotes one's life to reaching it. Happiness or unhappiness are by-products of one's striving.

NANCY
That's for a man—but for a woman it's different— Don't you agree, Sara?

SARA
Meaningfully.
A woman often finds happiness by accepting unhappiness.

NANCY
Rebellious.
No, I used to believe that but now I know it's a lie.

ELIZABETH
Well, I'm a woman and I quite agree with Jonathan. Happiness is beside the point. And when women talk of happiness I've always discovered they mean only one thing—love.

NANCY
Flustered.
Oh, no. I wasn't—I meant, everything.

ELIZABETH
I'm a woman and love isn't important to me.

JONATHAN
Take Ethan, now. He's an example of what I mean. He wants only one thing—to prove his power over the sea, which to him is life, to make the record, be at the top. I admire his will but I think his goal is nonsense. Still, the point is what does he care for happiness, his own or anyone else's—or for love?

NANCY
Objects violently.
Oh, no! You don't know Ethan as I know him. He's not the inhuman monster he makes himself out to be.

SARA
Comes to the rescue.
Nancy, you know you're not feeling very well. I think you should go to your cabin and lie down.
Nancy goes.
This calm and the stifling heat have affected her nerves.

ELIZABETH
With contempt.
She's a fool, that woman—a silly fool to show so plainly she's a fool.

WARREN
Teases her.
So old and wise and cryptic. What do you mean?

ELIZABETH
You know what I mean, Jonathan.

JONATHAN
Yes, I do.

ELIZABETH
It's all the fault of that horrible Mrs. Graber. Nancy talks to her. How can she. One should ignore her.

JONATHAN
Embarrassedly.
Oh, she's not so bad as I thought.

WARREN
She keeps to herself, minds her own business.

ELIZABETH
That's just what she doesn't do. I can feel her prying. And you can tell at a glance what she must have been, what she still is—

WARREN
Protests.
You can't say that—you've no proof.
Then, reprovingly.
Besides, what can you know of such things?

ELIZABETH
Nothing, of course, Father. I only mean she's evil. You understand, Jonathan.

JONATHAN
I understand it is best to ignore her, as you said.

ELIZABETH
Quickly.
Yes, of course, in practice I do. I haven't spoken a word to her. I cut her dead.

LEDA *comes forward on left to the end of the rail, turns to walk back.*

LEDA
Pleasantly.

Good evening.

MEN
Mutter.

Good evening.

Elizabeth stares at her with cold ferocity, fascinated.

LEDA
Returns the stare, then asks mockingly.

Yes? What do you want?

She laughs and walks back.

ELIZABETH
Breaks out furiously.

There! You see! She insults me continually with her disgusting—

WARREN
Impatiently.

You bring it on yourself. You deliberately provoke it. Why do you always stare at her like that? You were saying why doesn't Mrs. Payne ignore her. Why don't you?

ELIZABETH
Flustered.

I—I can't—there's something—I mean, look at her, you can't help seeing her.

WARREN

Don't look at her then.

He gets up.

It certainly is hot.

Sound of singing.

Is that Honey singing with the gold-seekers? Do you think he should, Jonathan?

54

JONATHAN
Laughs with affection.
Honey plays the clown, but he's a very shrewd fellow. He laughs, sings, jokes, and people tell him all he wants to know. He's going to the mines, so he's getting all the information they have.

DICKEY
That Graber is a worse influence than his wife, drunk and gambling all the time.

WARREN
I remember now where I heard his name. A bank upstate went bust. I suspect that is the same man off to seek a new fortune. Oh, this calm. I feel a foreboding. We seem to have escaped the curse of the first mate's death, but now—Damn it, if we'd only move!

ELIZABETH
It's all due to that woman's presence on board.

WARREN
Nonsense! Let's walk back and speak to the Captain.

> *Dickey and Warren go, Elizabeth and Jonathan follow.**

SARA
I think I'll stay here.
She thinks aloud.
Jonathan and Elizabeth seem to take to each other. Well, it'd be a good match for him. Evidently Ethan's not interested. But

---

* O'Neill's second thoughts (from the scenario):
   They go here leaving L[eda]. with Sara—scene between them—Eliz. goes below—scene between her & Nancy—Nancy to stateroom ("I thought you were going to stateroom to lie down")—Eliz. knocks on Ethan's door—he lets her in—scene between them with door open— Nancy comes out, jealous spying—Leda comes down, catches her—sends her away scornfully—wear heart on sleeve no way—Eliz. comes out— scene, for moment, her & Leda—then her & Ethan . . .—Nancy comes out—asks indignantly, what did you mean by saying that to me—then scene Nancy & Leda

Nancy's after him. She's making a fool of herself. I'll have to speak plainly to her.

> *Below,* NANCY *comes forward frightenedly to Ethan's door, wants to knock, hesitates.* LEDA *appears behind her.*

LEDA

I wouldn't do that if I were you. Never run after them. That's no way to play the game. At least, you've got to make them think they're running after you.

NANCY
Shocked, indignant.

I felt faint—heat—calm—only wanted to see if Ethan was awake because I want to ask him—

LEDA

About the weather? I know.

> *She waves this aside, asks impatiently.*

Why can't you be frank, then I might be able to help you get what you want? I'm all for women getting what they want from men.

NANCY

I—I don't know what you mean—I don't want anything.

LEDA

You want him. You want him to want you.

NANCY
Giving way.

No, I—he is—

LEDA

It's no good lying to me.

NANCY

Yes, I love him.

LEDA

Love? Well, I suppose that's as good a name for it as any other. You keep following me around. You want to be frank but you keep beating around the bush. What are you afraid of, that I'll think you're a bad woman? No women are bad to me except the fools that let men keep them from what they want.

NANCY

I'm afraid of your telling about the first mate.

LEDA

What? I tell? I've never squealed on anyone. And what is it to me? My only feeling is he was an ornery old crab and is better off dead. Don't tell me you're suffering from a guilty conscience?

NANCY

Yes—I see him lying there—in my dreams.

LEDA

Why? He would have died soon anyway—and, even if your Ethan—

NANCY

My Ethan?

LEDA

—Did want him out of his way in his heart, he never thought a smash in the face would do it.

NANCY

Yes, it was hitting his head, wasn't it? An accident.

LEDA

Forget it. I hate women with guilty consciences. It's too silly. Where do you think I would be if I harbored a conscience? I don't usually give a damn about other women's affairs but maybe it's being cooped up in this ship, what happened when I first came aboard. I feel all of us on the ship are mixed up, especially you and me. Maybe, tonight, it's the calm, the heat, that damned song and the sea that make me want to talk. I feel sorry for you. Like my own experience. Mine was a good family, in a small town, well off. My father owned carpet mills, died when I was a kid. I married a friend of my father's, following my mother's dying advice. He had handled my father's business. I was seventeen, just the age when girls get crushes on older men. He was thirty years older—hard, like my father. Then disillusion. He wanted money and my body. That shocked me then. Now I know it's all men ever want—although the two are usually separated.

NANCY

No!

LEDA

I grew to hate him. I got to feel like a young whore who was keeping an old pimp. It made me laugh, it was so idiotic. I used to lie in bed beside him and pray that he'd die, every night. I suppose you do that, too?

NANCY

No!

LEDA

Why not? It's only natural. I thought you were going to be frank.

NANCY

No—I—yes, I try not to—but I can't help—

LEDA

Of course you can't—any more than you can help wanting Ethan in bed with you instead.

NANCY

No.

Then, furiously.

Yes. I do. I do.

She weeps.

LEDA

Goes on.

One night I made up my mind if I was going to be a whore I was at least going to have some pleasure out of it, and make men pay for bringing me pleasure. So I left him and went to New York. Men have kept me ever since—not old men, young men. I've been able to pick and choose, and it's I who have always left them—until I had enough. I suppose you're wondering about Graber. Well, he's an exception, a reaction. I

don't give a damn about him but he's such a slob I felt sorry
for him.

NANCY

You make love into nothing but—bodies.

LEDA

And what else is it? And why not? Bodies are all right, aren't
they—healthy, natural? Aren't we animals? Can you go to bed
with a soul? Poetic drivel aside, love may start in heaven but
it goes on—or it dies—in bed. You want to go to bed with
Ethan, don't you—more than anything else in the world?

NANCY

No—yes, I do! I do!

LEDA

That's better. Why be ashamed of it? He's handsome. Well,
I'll help you. I know the game. He may be strange, different,
but he's a man. He's all wrapped up in himself, he's off in
the clouds. We've got to get him down to earth, get him to
see you not as a family friend but as a woman. Once he does,
you're pretty, you're still young looking. But it's your fault.
You've got to stop pretending to yourself and to learn you
must stop playing the family friend. Stay in the background.
You keep too near him. He can't see you. And I'll talk to
him, I'll bring his thoughts down to earth and flesh. Why do
you look like that? Don't you trust me? I don't want him. I
give you my solemn word as between women, I will do nothing
that isn't with the object of making him want you. Go to your
stateroom now. I'll wait and talk to him. You keep your door
open. Then when I'm finished you come out. Hurry now. It's
almost eight bells. I hear him moving around in there.

Nancy goes, then turns around.

NANCY

I—it isn't true—I couldn't—you've made me say things, think
things—

LEDA

All right. Blame me if you like, but go away.

NANCY
Bursts into tears.
I hate you. You're filthy.
She goes to her stateroom.

LEDA
But I notice she left the door open a little.
She sits waiting. [ETHAN *comes out of his cabin.*

ETHAN
Well, what do you want?

LEDA
I'll come in, if you like, and it won't cost you money. I'm on vacation, resigned, happily married—and you're not bad looking.

ETHAN
There's something about you as evil and unscrupulous as the sea—and as simple— You're partners in crime.

LEDA
Well, you love the sea, don't you? Are you afraid Nancy would be jealous?

ETHAN
Angry.
What do you mean?

LEDA
I suppose you'll tell me you're not sleeping with her?

ETHAN
Violently.
Of course I'm not! There's such a thing as honor.

LEDA
Skeptical and unimpressed.
You can't fool me.

ETHAN
Baffled.
What's the use!

60

LEDA

If not, then why not? A fool can see she wants you. You're doing her a wrong—[Don't act so disgusted. She may be a little older than you, but she's a pretty woman any man ought to want. But perhaps you're not much of a man. You'd have taken Hull's insult if it hadn't been for me.]*

He protests.

You're full of talk about the sea, but it teaches you to take what you want.

ETHAN
Impressed.

I suppose you're right.

LEDA

Why don't you pretend I'm her?

She kisses him.

*Ethan, in a rage, goes into his cabin and shuts the door.]***

The scene switches to the CAPTAIN above as he joins SARA.

PAYNE
Grumbling.

The passengers talk as if I could change the weather, make the wind blow.

Disappointed, but coldly satisfied.

This will teach your son Ethan. It's fate. That's the way the sea is. I had a foreboding, knew our luck couldn't last. A calm is unusual here. I'm not superstitious, but there was something strange about the first mate's death. Every time I go downstairs, I think of him and I'm afraid of slipping. I'm sorry I had to quarrel with Ethan. I really like the boy, but the ship comes before everything else. Something seems to be bothering him. Perhaps he's in love. Do you think he has his eye on Leda or Elizabeth?

---

* The bracketed words are taken from O'Neill's notes for the revision of the play.
** The entire bracketed scene is taken from O'Neill's second thoughts.

61

SARA
Encourages him.
I think it's probably Leda.

PAYNE
Approves, relieved.
Well, I'm glad. But I really want to talk to you about Nancy. She's been strange this trip. She seems unhappy. Has she confided in you?

SARA
No, she hasn't.

PAYNE
She seems to dislike me, as if I'd done something to offend her.

SARA
Maybe she feels that you're too much wrapped up in the ship, that you take her for granted.

PAYNE
That may be it. I've been worried, after all I'm getting old and she's still a young woman.

Eight bells. The scene switches.
ETHAN *comes out of his cabin, face to face with*
NANCY.

NANCY
Stammers.
I'm so frightened, this calm, there's something threatening about it.

Ethan takes her in his arms. Suddenly they kiss.
Then both sorry, guilty. He goes, rushes up to
deck to PAYNE *and* SARA.

PAYNE
Ah, there you are my boy. I've just been saying to your mother that I hoped you didn't take our quarrel too seriously. I'll leave you together.
He goes out.

SARA

What a good man he is!

ETHAN

Guilty.

To hell with his goodness!

Below NANCY *follows steps to companionway.*

NANCY

If he'd only fall—! Oh, I can't face him now, he'll want me
to go to bed with him, the fool, the disgusting old fool, he'll
never die. Oh, I want Ethan.

She rushes out to the main deck by the ladder.

ETHAN

To Sara, desperately.

This damned calm! The sea is so peaceful, I envy her.

Curtain

ACT THREE, SCENE TWO

Scene *Tenth day of the calm. The section of the clipper, from break of poop to end of wheelhouse, as seen from a point to starboard on main-deck level. The spanker and mizzensails are both set, spanker boom going off, left rear, mizzensail sheeted tight against starboard rail, extending diagonally off toward right, rear. The interior of the wheelhouse is revealed. On main deck, interior of Nancy's stateroom, cabin view, and Leda's stateroom. Discovered: on poop deck: in wheelhouse, the* HELMSMAN, CAPTAIN PAYNE, GRABER, *and* WARREN *playing cards; on deck near wheelhouse,* ELIZABETH *and* DICKEY; *on deck forward of mizzensail,* SARA *and* JONATHAN; *in Nancy's cabin,* NANCY; *in Leda's cabin,* LEDA *and* HONEY; *in recess,* WOLFE *playing solitaire.*

This scene should have the feeling of running simultaneously, a subject being picked up from one to another. It starts in Leda's stateroom, where she is just finishing dressing after having given herself to Honey.

The song of the gold-seekers, followed by a chanty.

LEDA
Pats Honey on the cheek, laughs.
Happy now, that you've got what you wanted? But I guess you're always happy anyway.

HONEY
Happy? Why shouldn't I be with the gift of your beautiful body, your—

LEDA

Laughs.

And of course that's all talk to make me feel it would be too low of me to mention money.

HONEY

Well, I don't have any anyway. But I'll find slews of gold in California and give you a hatful of nuggets.

LEDA

Laughs.

I like you. You'll get on. You'll promise people the moon and get them to give it to you.

HONEY

Grins.

I hope so.

LEDA

And you'll never have a guilty conscience. That's why I gave myself to you. You're refreshing—you get fun out of it and I get your fun and my own—so it's I who owe you something. You're the only one on this ship who doesn't want everything to be more than it is and doesn't blame himself because it isn't.

The song comes. Her nerves break.

Oh, curse that song! And curse the calm and the Captain!

Scene switches to the wheelhouse.

WARREN

Captain, make them stop that singing. If I were captain, I'd—

PAYNE

Hurt, but replies calmly.

The tempers of the crew and the gold-seekers are getting out of hand. Singing is a safety valve.

He turns to the helmsman.

Is there steerage way?

HELMSMAN

No, sir.

WARREN

No breeze yet?

PAYNE

No.

WARREN

And you don't even know where we are?

PAYNE

With no sun and no stars, we couldn't take a reading.

WARREN

You mean you haven't found a way. There's always a way, if you have will enough, concentration, drive to go ahead, if you're not too old and tired.

PAYNE

You're not young yourself, sir.

WARREN

A man is as old as he feels, sir.

[*The scene switches to* JONATHAN *and* LEDA.

LEDA

You know you ought to seduce Elizabeth and then she will have to marry you. You'll go far backed by her money and I wouldn't like to be in your way when you do get power.

JONATHAN

Thank you. But I'm afraid seducing Elizabeth just isn't possible. She's a pretty cold fish.

LEDA

What? You admit that anything is impossible—for you? You won't get as far as I thought.

JONATHAN

Stung.

No, but that isn't the way.

LEDA

You'll never get her any other way. You've got nothing but belief in yourself. You're the only man on board who attracts her because she sees you're attracted to her. I don't count the minister—to me he isn't a man. You've got to show her you want her, not her father's influence or money. It might be a good idea if you slept with me and she knew it.]*

> *The scene switches to* ELIZABETH *and* DICKEY. *The song of the gold-seekers continues in the background.*

ELIZABETH
Bursts out.

Damn their song!

DICKEY

Miss Warren!

ELIZABETH

A good Bible word—damn ship, damn cabin! I'm sorry. It's nerves. If only the sun would shine. Everything is dead. There's no present, no future, only the past, and that is dead too. I feel as if there was a fire inside me, as if I'd have to scream with pain.

DICKEY

I know. You must pray.

ELIZABETH

Pray? That's your business. I've lost faith in God.

DICKEY

You don't mean that.

> *He soothes her, strokes her arm amorously. She stares at him.*

> *The scene switches to* JONATHAN *and* SARA.

JONATHAN
Springs to his feet and looks over side.

Damn! We're actually going backwards! These tubs are at the mercy of nature. I want to live to see the day when they're wiped off the sea. I will, too. I'll help it along.

---

* The bracketed scene is taken from O'Neill's notes for the revision of the play.

I'm surprised to hear you talk like that. I always thought you had seawater in your veins.

He controls himself.

The only way is to forget the present, make plans for the future. I've noticed you making up to Elizabeth and I know she likes you. That'd be a good match.

JONATHAN

I know it would.

SARA

I think she's no feeling for Ethan and it's certain he's none for her.

JONATHAN

I don't care about that. I'm not looking for love. She has money, brains. This would be strictly a business proposition.

SARA

I think marriages are best that way.

JONATHAN

What are you worried about, Mother? Not about Honey making eyes at that trollop, are you? He isn't serious. He'll never be about anything.

SARA

You know it's not that.

JONATHAN

About Ethan and Nancy?

SARA

Yes.

JONATHAN

I am too. I'm afraid she'll make a fool of him. Too bad the old Captain can't die. That would solve matters.

SARA

Yes.

JONATHAN

The old fool! If he'd managed his ship right— He's too old. I'd like to see Ethan get his chance.

> *The scene switches back to* ELIZABETH *and* DICKEY.

ELIZABETH
Coldly.

I don't think even a minister should stroke a lady's arm that long.

DICKEY
Confused, embarrassed.

You said prayer was my business. But I have prayed—prayed and prayed to God.

ELIZABETH

What were you praying for? I have noticed you can't keep your eyes off that harlot when she's around.

DICKEY

Oh, no! Every soul is a soul to me. You have no right to judge. You may wrong her. She seems a mild, good-natured creature.

ELIZABETH

Rats! You know better! If you don't, you're a fool. She'll end up by committing fornication with every man on board, perhaps even including—

DICKEY

Miss Warren! Really, you forget—

ELIZABETH

I heard my father leave his stateroom last night and go to one across the cabin.

DICKEY

Oh, no. You must be wrong—I'm sure—

> *The scene switches to the wheelhouse.*

WARREN

As I said, a man is as old as he feels. I feel young. I am young in spirit, I could prove it to you by relating a little adventure—

He sneers at Graber.

—but perhaps it would be in bad taste in the presence of our friend here.

GRABER

Doesn't seem to hear, absentmindedly.

Will you bet, sir?

WARREN

Yes, by God, I insist on cutting. Your luck is too uncanny—and you don't know how to play, damn you. You make the stupidest mistakes, as if you wanted to lose. And yet you keep moving ahead of me. I'm not used to that, sir. I've always won. I've always beaten people. It's the cursed luck of this calm, this calm. The trouble with you, Captain, is your mind is not on the voyage. You're worrying about other things, your personal affairs, not your duty to the ship, its owner, its freight, its passengers—

PAYNE

Furious.

Sir, if you were not a passenger—

Controls himself.

I leave it to you to ask yourself if this is an honorable insult.

He turns and goes out.

WARREN

Sorry, I apologize.

Then in a loud voice to Graber.

He's too old, too old to be captain of this ship, too old to be a husband. He ought to resign, step down, let young Harford try and get us out of this mess.

GRABER

He'll hear you—but I suppose you want him to.

WARREN

Yes. Something must be done. We can't just sit back and grow old in this calm of death. But let's play. What card did I lead? I'll confess I don't like cards. I don't like losing. I don't like you. I'm only playing to avoid my daughter. She suspects—never mind what, only this night, you see. I don't know what

70

young girls are coming to. In my generation, a girl would have died of shame rather than let such a thought enter her head, especially about her father.

Confidentially.

Listen, Graber. In this strange situation we're in, we might be frank, eh? Tell me now, you're not really married to Leda, are you?

GRABER

No.

WARREN

Ah, I thought not, sir. Otherwise, your calm would be hard to understand.

GRABER

I asked her to marry me but she wouldn't have me.

WARREN

Ah, well, nothing to say to that. My play, isn't it? Let me see—

The scene switches to DICKEY *and* ELIZABETH.

ELIZABETH

I am not mistaken. He went to her stateroom. I tell you she is turning this ship into a brothel. I will wager there's a man in her stateroom right now.

DICKEY

Loosens his collar.

It's really stifling tonight. Miss Warren, I know my profession hasn't much to offer.

Bitterly.

God doesn't pay very well. I think in California I may go to the mines, in fact if you say the word, I would do anything, for you are very beautiful and disturbing, and I love you.

ELIZABETH

Scornfully.

Don't be a fool! I am through with love. I will marry a man of brains and ability who will be rich, whom I can help with my brains to become rich. That is all I care for now. I am afraid that whore has possessed you as she has everyone, almost. I advise you to take your proposal to her.

> *Then, violently.*

It is all the fault of this fool of a captain. If he would keep a decent discipline on his ship— But how can you expect a man who is too old and weak even to control his own wife—?

DICKEY

You think she—?

ELIZABETH

With Ethan—of course.

DICKEY

Yes, I admit her actions are exceedingly suspicious. Yes, he is a weak character, he—

> *Sees Captain.*

Ssshh!

> *He tries to lead her back.*

ELIZABETH

> *Breaks away.*

No. I am going forward to find Mr. Jonathan Harford, a man of brains and ability—and please don't follow me. Go below to Leda.

> *She goes forward to* JONATHAN *and* SARA. *Dickey avoids the Captain and goes astern around rear corner of the wheelhouse.*
>
> *The scene switches to the* CAPTAIN, *standing over Nancy's room.*

PAYNE

> *Thinks.*

She's innocent, I swear, but still—and that Ethan!

> *Hopelessly.*

I feel that Nancy loves him.

> *The scene switches to Nancy's room.*

NANCY

I can't sleep. I long for Ethan. Oh, why doesn't he take me. We've both pretended long enough. What a terrible thing to

say, when the poor old man loves me so. But what do I care?
I hate him. I hate him.

> *Horrified.*

What am I saying? I'm no better than a whore like Leda!

> *The scene switches to* LEDA *and* HONEY.

HONEY
> *Jokingly.*

I hope you got a good price from Warren last night.

LEDA

Yes, and I put it in his mind to play cards with Ben. Ben's
having a run of luck and he gives me all his winnings.

HONEY

I never saw such luck.

LEDA

Unlucky at love, eh? Funny thing is he wants to love. He has
a guilty conscience. He committed a big sin, never mind what,
for me, and is only playing and drinking so as not to think.

HONEY

Do you suppose Nancy and Ethan have been to bed together?

LEDA

I don't know. I hope so for her sake.* Your brother is inhuman.

HONEY

Yes, he's faithful to the sea. He's crazy.

LEDA

What about Wolfe?

HONEY
> *Laughs.*

There's one you'd never get. No use hoping.

LEDA

He and I'd be a perfect couple. He gives as little a damn
about anything as I do.

---

* O'Neill's second thoughts (from the scenario):
> & for captain's sake—what do you mean—nothing—

They go out just as ETHAN *comes out of his state-room at rear. He sees them and comes forward to* WOLFE *in the recess. Wolfe is endlessly practicing shuffling.* HONEY *joins them.*

ETHAN
With bitter contempt, to Honey.
It must be fine to be nothing but a belly and a sexual organ.

HONEY
Grins, unembarrassed.
It is, surely. But you don't do me justice. I've a most melodious singing voice, too.

ETHAN
And the gift of plausible gab.

HONEY
Don't disparage that, for you'll find you'll need it before long. The boys up forward are getting hot and unless a breeze comes soon— It's lucky for the Captain I'm not unscrupulous.

ETHAN
You?

HONEY
I could get myself elected captain this minute. Think that over. As for lying with Leda, isn't a living woman better to love than the sea or a damned wooden tub? I advise you to try Leda. In her arms you can forget your dream of a record.
Ethan is disgusted.
Wolfe, when are you going to put your card practice to use? You ought to join the game upstairs. Graber's luck won't last. You can make some money. I'll back you. You won't? Afraid, are you?

Wolfe is stung. Honey adds another taunt and goes out entrance to main deck, singing.

The scene switches to SARA, JONATHAN, *and* ELIZABETH.

74

SARA
Calls to Honey.
Don't you be getting drunk!

HONEY
Who? Me? Why, Mother!

SARA
Laughs.
He's a fine lad at heart. Where has he been all this time, I
wonder?

ELIZABETH
Down with Leda. You should complain to the Captain, Mrs.
Harford. She is corrupting your son.

SARA
Leda can't corrupt anyone who doesn't want to be corrupted.

ELIZABETH
Primly.
I disagree. She's a very evil woman. She puts thoughts in your
head, I mean in men's heads.

> *The scene switches to the* CAPTAIN *and* DICKEY.
> LEDA *stands at the rail by the sail.*

DICKEY
The calm is the punishment of God for the sin on this ship
and that woman is the cause of it all. You should speak to
her, Captain. It's your duty.

PAYNE
Why not yours?

DICKEY
To be truthful, I'm afraid of her. She's beautiful. She wouldn't
believe me. I'm too young. But you are an old man, old enough
to be her father.

PAYNE
Stung.
I'm as old as I feel. I'm young. I'm strong. I could break you
over my knee with one hand. I'm not afraid to speak to her.

He goes over to Leda.

Young woman, I won't have all this carrying on on my ship,
I—

LEDA
Smiles.

You talk like an old man, Captain. What would your wife
think to hear you talking such old man's talk? She wouldn't
love you anymore. But I know that silly old shy priest put it
in your head, because you're not old. You're young in spirit.
A man is as old as he feels. I'm sure you feel young—worth
two young men.

He gives way.

You're not old to me.

PAYNE

If I were not a married man in love with my wife, I would ask
you to let me come to your stateroom.

LEDA

All right, I'll expect you. But it will cost you money.

PAYNE

It doesn't cost the young money.

Sharply.

Remember I've warned you. No more monkey business on my
ship.

*Leaves her, moves back to rail near wheelhouse.
Leda laughs.*

The scene switches to SARA, JONATHAN, *and*
ELIZABETH.

ELIZABETH
Looks back.

There's that harlot now, coming forward. Let's go to the stern.

JONATHAN

Come on, Mother. We need the exercise.

They come back.

LEDA
Meets Elizabeth's stare.
Why hate me? Men would want you, too, if you'd only give them a chance.

ELIZABETH
Whore!

LEDA
Don't be so envious!

JONATHAN
To Elizabeth.
I thought you were going to ignore her.
He takes her away. Sara stops.

SARA
To Leda.
You're right. She has no more blood than a fish. But she's rich. Jonathan must marry her—
Guiltily.
God forgive me, why am I telling such thoughts to you?

LEDA
For God's sake, don't you get a guilty conscience, too. You can't fool me. You're a real woman. You want to get what you want.

Sara goes astern. Leda goes forward. The CAP-
TAIN *stands above.*

PAYNE
Thinks.
I am old. I really want to die. I sought to slip on the stairs.
He goes into the wheelhouse.

The scene switches to Nancy's stateroom.

NANCY
Thinks.
I wish he would die.

Leda goes down the ladder.

The scene switches to WOLFE *and* ETHAN.

77

ETHAN

Bursts out exasperatedly.

What are you after, Wolfe? Does the calm mean anything to you? Don't you love anything?

WOLFE

No, I keep out of the game.

ETHAN

You and I used to have something underneath in common—something of our father—but now I feel you're lost—and I need to talk to someone.

WOLFE

Warms a little.

But what can I say to you? You don't want wisdom, I see in your heart.

ETHAN

What is wisdom?

WOLFE

You have a great power of love. I envy you. I can't love. You could so easily be happy. I have had to put happiness aside and not be interested in it. You could love a ship without desiring to own it, you could love the sea without desiring to conquer it, you could love yourself without desiring to destroy yourself.

ETHAN

Fiercely.

A eunuch's philosophy! No. Possessions, power—those are the things that count.

WOLFE

Then why don't you possess Nancy?

ETHAN

Honor.

WOLFE

Yes, exactly.

ETHAN

Grows bitter.

I'm coming to the point where I believe all dreams are non-sense.

WOLFE

Yes, they are—but look out you don't substitute other non-sense for them.

ETHAN

I might as well rush back into Leda's arms, become an animal like Honey.

WOLFE

That's the other nonsense.

ETHAN

You're a live dead man.

WOLFE

I accept fate.

ETHAN

I'll make fate.

He goes out. Sees Leda.

LEDA

Why don't you take Nancy?

ETHAN

No, there's guilt there. Possession. I want to let go, go down, drown, forget—

He kisses her.

LEDA

No. I don't love you. You want love. You can't evade your conscience and get what you want by sleeping with me and pretending I'm Nancy.

She approaches Wolfe in his recess.

You're the only man I really want to sleep with on this ship and you scorn me.

WOLFE

No, not you—it's the game. I refuse to play.

LEDA

I'd like to see what you're made of. I will, too, some day.

> *She goes to Nancy's room.*
> *Ethan outside Wolfe's recess is disturbed for a second. He thinks.*

ETHAN

I do want to use Leda for Nancy, to escape in phantoms.
> *He enters the recess.*

Where's Leda?

WOLFE

Gone to her room, I suppose. Look out for that other nonsense.

> *Ethan goes to Leda's room, finds Nancy. She gets implications why he came there. Cries. The room has its effect on both. They kiss.*

NANCY

No. Honor. We must wait.

> *Eight bells sounds.*
> *Ethan goes out to go on deck by companionway. Nancy goes back to her own room. Ethan goes to the wheelhouse, relieves the Captain. Nancy below, death wish. Captain starts down stairs, death fear, death longing. Ethan watching, death wish. Captain goes lower. Nancy calls, denying death wish, "Be careful on the stairs!" The Captain falls. Nancy shrieks. The others crowd into the pilothouse.*

ETHAN

Stand back!

> *He goes down, drags Captain into Nancy's cabin.*

NANCY

Is he——?

ETHAN

Yes, I think he's dead.

> *They stare at each other. She clasps him passionately in her arms.*

80

NANCY

Oh, Ethan, everything is all right now!

Payne groans. Nancy, with utter despair.

Oh, he isn't dead!

ETHAN

Starts to curse, controls himself, bends by the body, then straightens up.

No.

They stare at each other over the body, the same idea coming to each.

NANCY

They know he fell. They'd never know—

ETHAN

Gives in, then recoils.

Good God, are you mad?

NANCY

Denies.

I—I don't know what you mean—what did you think I meant —I only thought I read something in your mind—

ETHAN

I?—Good God, no!—yes, why should I lie to you?—for a moment I thought—against my will—but it's too infamous— come—we must get him to bed—

NANCY

Yes, yes—I'll nurse him. I'll do anything.

Payne groans, moves.

ETHAN

To Payne.

You'll be all right, sir. Just a bad fall. You slipped.

NANCY

Kisses Payne.

Yes, my dear husband. I'll take care of you and make you well.

Curtain

81

ACT THREE, SCENE THREE

Scene   *Looking forward from after-end of wheelhouse at level of the main deck, showing interior of wheelhouse on poop deck, and interiors of after-cabin below, Sara's cabin at left, Captain's cabin at right.*

It is the twentieth day of the calm.

In the wheelhouse are WARREN *and* GRABER *playing cards,* WOLFE *looking on, standing,* ETHAN *by the man at the wheel, staring out of the open door. At left of the wheelhouse are* ELIZABETH *and* DICKEY. *Below, in Sara's state-room, are* SARA *and* JONATHAN. *In Captain's cabin at right he lies in bunk with his eyes closed.* NANCY *sits beside his bed with her eyes fixed on his face.*

In the wheelhouse the scene repeats the pattern of the previous scenes except that everyone is more hectic.

WARREN
Flies into rage.

You're cheating against yourself, Graber! No gentleman would do that. It's humiliating to me. Do you think I'm such a bad loser?

WOLFE
He's not thinking of you but of himself.

WARREN
If you want to get in the game, say so.

WOLFE

No.

Then shut up! Wanting to lose indeed! Preposterous—inhuman
—crazy—but I think we're all going crazy in this damned
calm. Well, Ethan, so you finally got the sun today only to find
that we're fifty miles behind where we were two weeks ago! A
fine record, young man—you with your talk of records—

ETHAN

I must remind you, sir, I am not in command of this ship.

WARREN

Yes, of course. Still you might do something.

ETHAN

The Captain still gives the orders.

WARREN

By God, I'm not superstitious, but I think he's a Jonah. I
wish—but of course I don't mean that. Poor old fellow! He
can't help being old, left behind his time. By the way, how
is he?

ETHAN

Better, his wife says. He's resting easily.

The scene switches to the Captain's cabin.
NANCY *is staring in front of her. The* CAPTAIN
*opens his eyes and reads her look. She senses
it and looks at him and starts guiltily.*

NANCY
Frightenedly.
Enoch! Why are you staring at me like that? What do you
want of me? You stare as if you were waiting—
He closes his eyes.
You're better, dear. Ethan says you're much better. I'm so
happy, dear.

The scene switches back to the wheelhouse.

WARREN

So he's better, is he? A miraculous recovery—and he owes it
all to that sweet woman—the way she's nursed him—a lesson

to all. She never sleeps. You haven't slept much yourself in
the past ten days, I'll wager, Captain.

ETHAN

I am not Captain. No, I haven't slept much. It isn't a situation
where one craves for sleep much.
He suddenly turns on Wolfe fiercely.
For God's sake, stop your infernal pacing! I never saw you so
restless before. Why don't you sit down, join in the game, do
something!

> *He turns and strides out, comes to the rail over
> the Captain's stateroom.*

> *The scene switches to* ELIZABETH *and* DICKEY.

ELIZABETH

Looking in the cabin window.
There is something strange about that Wolfe. I admire him—
and I despise him. I admire him because he's the only man on
board that whore, Leda, can't influence, and I despise him
because I feel in him an indifference to women so insulting.
By the way, where is that Leda? Up with the crew and the gold-
seekers, I suppose. She'll have had every man on ship before
we get to California. And in there her husband or keeper sits
playing. My God, it's all so mad, this calm!

DICKEY

I've prayed and prayed to God for wind, Miss Warren. But perhaps He sees that my heart is no longer pure.

ELIZABETH

You mean you too have been with Leda? I guessed it, seeing
you no longer paw my arm.

DICKEY

Yes, I confess last night I talked with her and everything suddenly became innocent and clear to me. It did not matter what
I did. There was no sin, no God. Life was innocent and beautiful, without guilt.

I wish she could make me feel that! Oh, it's so hot! I'm stifling!
That damned song! I wish she would come back. I hate her.
I'd like to kill her, but at least when she's around I feel alive.

DICKEY

But today I know there must be a God, and this calm, it is all
his vengeance on me for my evil heart.

ELIZABETH

You fool, you are not that important. You are only half a
man. Was I flattered when you pawed my arm? No, it only
annoyed me. That's proof, isn't it? I'm sure Leda would tell
you it was.

DICKEY

Then you think it wasn't important? Oh, thank you, I am so
glad, so glad!
He cries.

ELIZABETH

Fool! Nothing you can do could be important! I am beginning
to believe with Leda that nothing matters except to want and
to be wanted. If I could only want!
She looks in the window.
Look at my father for a moral lesson. I have watched him. He
has been cheating for days now. It is the infallible system on
which he has built his success. But now it loses, although the
other cheats himself and tries to lose. Oh, Father, how God
must laugh at you behind your back!
She laughs.

In the wheelhouse.

WARREN
Bangs his fist on the table.
Your game again. This passes all bounds, sir!
Then, in another tone.
Have you any children?
Graber doesn't answer.
You should thank God, sir. I have a daughter. It is a worse
form of slavery than being a husband, this being a father, and,

by God, I'm sick of it. I'll marry her off, if I can only get a man to want her. Men are attracted to her at first because she's beautiful like her mother, but they soon guess that, like her mother, she's as cold as a dead fish!

Back to ELIZABETH *and* DICKEY.

ELIZABETH
Turns away from the window with a sobbing cry.
It's a lie, isn't it? Tell me it's a lie. Jonathan, he loves me, he wants me, doesn't he? You must have noticed the way he looks at me, and it isn't for my money, is it?

DICKEY
Looking in at the game.
I am beginning to think that, after all, gambling is no sin. I'd like to play, but I have no money. The ministry is the most ill-paid calling. Of course, if you were sure of a reward hereafter for doing without in this world—sure of the justice of God—but in this calm one doubts. Perhaps God cares nothing about justice for man. I thought it would be a very good thing for me if I could marry you, Elizabeth, with your money and position—the food I could eat, for example—I am very greedy —but I didn't want you—too cold—and so I couldn't make you want—

ELIZABETH
In a rage.
So, even you—! You dare to tell me that, you pitiful creature, you!

She slaps his face and turns to go forward just as LEDA *comes back. She stands staring at Leda.*

LEDA
Laughs.
Good! I didn't think you had it in you. Perhaps, having gone that far you'll be frank at last and tell me what you want from me.

ELIZABETH
Want from you? Is it likely I would want anything from a whore like you?

LEDA

Yes—professional advice—secrets of the trade. You have wished to sell yourself, but before you can sell, you must make men want.

ELIZABETH

Many of them have wanted—

LEDA

Your hand in marriage for your money? But that's not what you want them to want. You don't want to buy them. You want to make them buy you.

ELIZABETH
Grows confidential.

Yes, to be candid, I have fallen a little in love with Jonathan. But he is so cold, I think he may be only after my money.

LEDA

Well, give yourself to him.

ELIZABETH

Give myself!

LEDA

Find out if he wants you—if you want him.

ELIZABETH

But that's disgusting! Still, I see what you mean. If I let him seduce me—he seems like a man of honor—I would have him then.

LEDA
Laughs scornfully.

You need no advice from me. I need advice from you, for I'm still so impractical as to give myself for nothing now and then. But you don't fool me. You are only hiding from yourself your fear that men do not want you because they feel you cannot give yourself.

ELIZABETH

I can! I will!

LEDA

Then prove it.

She laughs, starts to go into the wheelhouse.

DICKEY
Grabs her arm, whispers.

You are so right, Miss Leda. What shall it profit a man if he give you up for a supposition like his soul? I shall visit you again tonight, if I may.

Leda laughs and goes into the wheelhouse.

In the wheelhouse.

WARREN

You have cleaned me out of all available cash, Graber. I shall have to stop.

GRABER

I'll give it all back to you and we'll play again. You may win.

LEDA
Laughs.

Still winning with a guilty conscience, Ben?

GRABER

Yes, I have no luck, Leda.

WARREN
Outraged.

What kind of man is he to make such an offer? Does money mean nothing? It's a sacred responsibility. You're a criminal scoundrel, sir, who ought to be in a lunatic asylum.
Then, shrewdly.

But it is the duty of a sound businessman to remove money from irresponsible quarters. I accept your offer—but, of course, as a debt of honor between us.

From outside, Elizabeth laughs mockingly.

LEDA
Taunts Wolfe.

Still afraid to get in the game, Wolfe? But I see you've at least come up to watch it. That's something.

WOLFE

It means nothing.

LEDA

No?

She laughs, goes out rear. Wolfe sits down at the table.

Outside the wheelhouse.

ELIZABETH

That lying whore! I'll prove to her I can give as well as she.

DICKEY

Yes, it's better to give than receive.

ELIZABETH

Jonathan is below, I think—perhaps in his stateroom alone.
She goes.

Dickey enters the wheelhouse.

DICKEY

I was like you once, Wolfe. I thought gambling was a sin, but now—

Wolfe stares at him for a second, coldly. Dickey shrinks away, muttering.

I beg your pardon. My mistake.

LEDA comes up to ETHAN at the rail over the Captain's stateroom. He does not notice her at first.

ETHAN

Thinks.

What fools we were when we had that chance! No one would have suspected.

Then, guiltily.

Good God! What am I thinking! Murder!

The scene switches to NANCY below.

NANCY

Staring at Payne.

What fools we were when we had that chance! No one would have suspected.

Then, guiltily.

Oh, no! What am I thinking? Murder!

Then, repentantly, to Payne.

Tell me you feel better, dear. I love you. You're such a good husband. I would do anything for you.

The scene switches back to ETHAN *and* LEDA.

LEDA

To Ethan.

Why have a guilty conscience? You love this ship, you love Nancy. Of course you wish he'd die. You'd like to kill him. It's only natural.

ETHAN

Automatically.

Yes. I know it's silly to feel guilty. I know we were damned fools—

Then, with a shudder, staring at Leda.

But one doesn't admit such thoughts.

LEDA

Why doesn't one? I admit everything—and everyone.

ETHAN

You're a horrible woman.

LEDA

You said I was like the sea.

ETHAN

The sea is horrible to me now. What is it waiting for so contemptuously and surely? What are you waiting for?

LEDA

I? For your brother Wolfe to desire me.

ETHAN

You'll wait a long time!

90

LEDA

I've fallen in love with him. Don't you think he will ever cease being indifferent? His indifference makes me despise myself, I feel dirty, and so to lull my guilty conscience, I drown myself in mere lust. But it's no good. No! I don't love him! I hate him for making me despise myself. I have built my life on desire for my body, but it is nothing to him, he doesn't want me, and so I'm becoming his slave. But I'll win in the end.

ETHAN

Love? You speak of love? You mean lust, don't you?

LEDA

I've never noticed much difference.

ETHAN

You don't know what love means.

LEDA

You don't! For example, if Wolfe loved me and he were married to an old fool he didn't love, do you suppose I'd hesitate a moment to murder for love? Lust is what you've the guts to do to get it.

ETHAN

I'm going down to see how the Captain is.

LEDA

I hear he's better.

ETHAN

Yes.

LEDA

And you haven't possessed Nancy yet?

ETHAN

I only want what can be mine.

LEDA

Laughs.

Poor Nancy! Well, I hope the murder will be soon. I hate this calm.

91

She goes. Ethan is left alone. He thinks.

ETHAN

I stopped Nancy. She was going to— It was I who stopped her— She had more courage than I—

The scene switches to NANCY *and* CAPTAIN.

PAYNE

I don't want to get well. I want to die—and you know the reason. I'm dead already. You've murdered me.

NANCY

No, don't say that, Enoch! It's not true!

The scene switches to JONATHAN *and* SARA.

JONATHAN

Yes, it might be a very good match for me. I can use Warren in my plans. But I think he thinks we have some money and when he finds out I've nothing in that line to offer, he'll refuse his consent, and as she's under his thumb—

SARA

You think so. I don't. If she loved you—

JONATHAN

Let's not talk of love. She wants to get married to get away from her father, but she cares nothing for love. She's as cold as ice.

SARA

Well then, I'm sure at least she wants to believe you love her. I think you've been too respectful with her.

JONATHAN

I see. There's something in what you say, but not what you mean. Supposing, for example, I could seduce her—

SARA

I won't have that kind of talk!

JONATHAN

I'm not talking to you as my mother but as the head of the firm.

92

SARA

You've no heart in you.

JONATHAN

Smiles.

Do you want me to make a good match or don't you?

> *The scene switches to the after-cabin.* LEDA *and*
> ELIZABETH *just coming out of Jonathan's room.*

ELIZABETH

He isn't there. I waited but he didn't come—or I would have
proved to you—

LEDA

Good for you. You're coming alive at last.

Puts her arm around her.

Let's go in to see how the Captain is, and let Nancy get out
of there for a while. She's killing herself nursing that old fool.

ELIZABETH

It must be terrible being married to an old man when you love
someone else.

LEDA

Yes, I'd murder him.

ELIZABETH

Yes, so would I.

LEDA

Laughs.

You *are* being born.

ELIZABETH

Yes, I think you are the only one on board who knows what life
is about. You—you will teach me, won't you—now that I've
been frank with you?

LEDA

You don't need me now. You can teach yourself.

> *They knock at the door of the Captain's state-*
> *room.*

NANCY
Startled.

Come in.

They enter.

ELIZABETH

We've come to persuade you to take a little walk with us—a change.

NANCY

No, I must stay here.

PAYNE

Go ahead. It's no use waiting. I'm not going to die tonight.

The three women go out. They meet HONEY, *coming from forward, drunk, with bottle. He greets them uproariously, kisses Leda.* SARA *and* JONATHAN *come out.*

ELIZABETH

You must kiss me, too, Honey—but no, I'd rather kiss Jonathan.

She does so.

HONEY

Oho, so that's how the land lies! I've misjudged you. I thought you were a dried up stick.

ELIZABETH

Well, I'm not, am I, Jonathan? I went looking for you in your room just now. I waited, but you didn't come.

JONATHAN

I'll be there later.

ELIZABETH

I'll remember.

HONEY

The gold-seekers and the crew have made me a committee of one to demand that the Captain resign all power to Ethan. I've convinced the fools that the Captain's a Jonah, that as soon as he's out, the ship will move. And if it doesn't, I'll tell them it *is* moving and they'll believe it! I ought to be a politician! Come on, let's drink, ladies, and then Jonathan and I will deliver the message.

NANCY

You can't! The shock would kill him.

HONEY

And wouldn't that be a blessing?

NANCY

You're horrible.
Bursts into tears, then, fiercely.
Yes! It would!

They drink. Honey and Jonathan go into the Captain's stateroom.

HONEY

Captain Payne, the gold-seekers and the crew have elected me a committee to demand that you resign command of the ship to Ethan—

PAYNE
Flies into a rage.
What! Give up the ship! Never!

The scene switches to the wheelhouse above.

ETHAN
Thinks.
I will—I'll kill him!
He goes out of the wheelhouse and comes down the stairs.

HONEY

Well, Ethan, the gold-seekers and the crew have voted to demand that the Captain turn over the ship to you, but Payne refuses.

ETHAN

Of course he's the Captain and will continue so. I'll shoot down anyone who says differently.

95

*Honey and Jonathan go to the wheelhouse to get
others to come down to the party.*

HONEY
Philosophically.
I'll tell them it's done. They'll believe me.
In the wheelhouse he hands the bottle around.

*In the Captain's stateroom, Ethan gets the Cap-
tain to bed.*

PAYNE
Thank you, Ethan, for your loyalty. I'm afraid I've misjudged
you. I see I can count on your loyalty in all things. You
haven't slept with Nancy, have you?

ETHAN
No.

PAYNE
At last I can sleep.

ETHAN
Yes.

*The scene switches to the after-cabin. The
women are having a party.*

LEDA
Let's be frank. There are no men around with their codes and
pretences that we have to pretend to believe in. We can confess
our ruthless lust for giving ourselves to power. The spirit is of
no importance, it's the body that counts.

*The others nod their heads in agreement. This
alternates with the men's party in the wheelhouse. Then the scene switches to the Captain's
stateroom.*

ETHAN
Whispers.
Are you asleep, sir?

PAYNE

Just slipping off. I'm so peaceful now that I know. I'm old.
You can wait for Nancy—the ship—

He begins to go to sleep.

Why do you look at me like that? Never mind. I'm tired. I
want to sleep and forget.

*The scene switches back to the women's party.
Nancy gets up.*

NANCY

Ruthless and cruel.

I'm sick of this calm, this death in life, this waiting. I want
what I can take from life, now!

*She goes into the Captain's stateroom, sees Ethan
advancing with a pillow, says fiercely, "No! Give
me what is mine!" She snatches the pillow from
his hands, leaps at Payne, and shoves the pillow
over his face.*

Outside, the three women are of one mind.

LEDA

Men talk a lot about love, the fools, and make poetry to laud
it because they're all afraid to face it.

*The others nod their heads in agreement. Up in
the wheelhouse, Honey is singing. Suddenly all
join in the song of the gold-seekers, even the
women downstairs.*

THE THIRD MATE *comes in.*

THIRD MATE

There's a squall coming. Maybe it means wind.

He shouts down to Ethan.

Oh, Mr. Harford!

Curtain

97

ACT FOUR, SCENE ONE

Scene *Late January, late afternoon, approaching Golden
Gate. A gentle warm wind comes from starboard.
The scene shows the after-section of the ship
viewed from the starboard as in Scene Two of
Act Three, but no interiors are revealed. Mizzensail diagonal from left, rear to off right front.
All passengers are on deck except Graber and
Wolfe, all in a hectic tense state of excitement
and jubilation.* DICKEY, WARREN, JONATHAN, *and*
HONEY *are sitting by the first deckhouse forward
from the wheelhouse;* SARA, NANCY, ELIZABETH,
and LEDA *are sitting grouped by the mast at the
break of the poop. But these groups are not
fixed. They are all restless. They keep rising, sitting down, the groups intermingle.*

*As the curtain rises, all are talking excitedly
about being almost in sight of land.*

WARREN

I'm sure we'll beat the *Flying Cloud*'s record. The wind has
died down a bit, but it's from astern and we're hours ahead of
the record.

*Remarks are heard from each group, rising above
the chatter.*

NANCY

What a voyage we've had! There were times when I felt we
were so close to death. I never saw such storms. We've lived
life at its highest, and it's Ethan who has pulled us through.
He's driven the ship as she's never been driven before, he is a
superman, he has beaten the sea.

SARA

How lucky the old Captain died when he did! We've almost
forgotten him. It's hard to remember that he was ever on the

ship. The Reverend Mr. Dickey married Ethan and Nancy right after he had said the burial service over Captain Payne, almost like a double ceremony!

ELIZABETH

There was nothing strange in that, it was what Nancy wanted. Of course she didn't want to wait. She had never loved the Captain, she was glad he was dead. She loved Ethan, it was all so natural.

> *Behind, as a background, is the triumphant song of the gold-seekers, dominating a subdued, beaten sea chanty, and the clanking of the pump, for the ship has been driven so hard that she is leaking badly.*

> *The sentences and exclamations come from both groups at first, then a topic is taken up by one group, then by the other.*

WARREN
Chuckles.

That pump is sure clanking away, the leaking must be worse. Ethan has wracked my ship to bits, she won't be worth a damn, but I can have her tinkered up to run okay and on the strength of this record, depression or no depression, I can sell her to England for a good price.

> *Dickey laughs. Jonathan and Honey approve. Everyone is totally immoral.*

JONATHAN
To the women.

Warren says Ethan may have ruined his ship but the record will mean he can sell it to England, even so, at a good price.

SARA

That's a good businessman for you. If your father had only had some business resource—

ELIZABETH

I'm proud of my father. That's just like him, he had no honor, he'd cheat the devil.

NANCY

Keeps going back to the wheelhouse to kiss Ethan, in a trance of passionate love. To the others.

You don't know what it means to be tied down to an old man.

WARREN

Of course, he was ten years older than me—I'm young.

NANCY

It was such a relief when he died.

She leaves them to return to the women.

WARREN

"When he died!" I guess we all have a strong suspicion the old fool's departure was speeded, eh? But never mind, we'll let the happy lovers keep their little secret.

JONATHAN

It's a fine victory for Ethan. You should want and get what you want. The end justifies the means.

DICKEY

Of course. It is written that God works in mysterious ways. It would be difficult to justify His means, eh?

JONATHAN

Still and all, Ethan's end is a dead thing. Sail is dead. This was good as a last romantic gesture. Ethan would make a great success if he only didn't have the touch of the poet in him.

WARREN

Demurs.

Don't be so sure, young man. I begin to believe sail may still have a future, after this record.

The scene shifts to the women's group.

SARA

Well, it was a duel between Ethan and the sea and he's beat it. My father was a great duelist, and it's the touch of the poet in Ethan that he gets from both sides of the family that makes him dream great dreams of himself as a hero of old and follow his dreams to the end.

100

NANCY

Yes, he is a poet, a great poet of love.

ELIZABETH

Yes, one's love must be a poet or he doesn't know how to love. Jonathan is a poet, too, in his way.

SARA

I hope now that Ethan has beaten the sea, he'll give it up, will dream of wealth and power on land and get that, too. It's more satisfying, for you can't hold the sea, it runs through even a poet's fingers.

ELIZABETH

That's Jonathan's dream. Ethan and he will work together.
Kisses Nancy.
You and I will be like sisters and Sara will be our mother and we will help our men take possession of the world—and we will possess the world by possessing them.

SARA

Have you and Jonathan spoken to your father? Jonathan is so poor. Your father may object.

ELIZABETH

Laughs.
He can't object now. You have guessed that, surely. Father wouldn't want a scandal. And that reminds me, we're forgetting all about Leda. She must be one of us and she will be. Her eye is on Wolfe, and what Leda wants she takes.

SARA

I hope so. It would wake him up.

ELIZABETH

We all ought to be so grateful to her. I feel we owe her so much. I know I do. I love her. I bless the day I met her. She taught me how to awake, soul and body. I was so warped in myself, so dead, so sick. She makes everything so simple and innocent, you see just what you want, you take it.

NANCY

Yes. She speaks and you forget guilt.

101

SARA

Yes, she's a good woman at heart. She wants everyone to be happy, to have what they want.

ELIZABETH

Where is she?

SARA

She's in the wheelhouse, watching Graber and Wolfe play. Wolfe is winning all Graber's money and Graber is so pleased, but Wolfe is indifferent. He isn't human.

ELIZABETH

Oh, Leda will make him human. She did me and I was as cold as he is, almost.

Jonathan comes to get Elizabeth.

JONATHAN

Come, Elizabeth. Now is a good time to speak to your father. He's a little tipsy, in a genial mood.

He and Elizabeth approach Warren and Dickey.

WARREN

So you've come, eh? Don't go, Dickey. This will mean a job for you soon. I suppose I ought to tell you to wait, Jonathan, prove yourself first, get some money. My daughter is still young, she's the prop of my declining years.

ELIZABETH

Laughs.

But I'm not your prop! You want to get free of me. And anyway it's too late to think of waiting.

WARREN

Oh, so? Well, I confess I guessed as much. I suppose I ought to curse you—but that's a lot of nonsense. I understand the hot blood of youth.

DICKEY

The end is propagation, so the particular means is always justified.

ETHAN *comes out and receives cheers and questions from all.*

ETHAN

Looks up at the sails, frowns for a second, then reassured.

We won't beat the record by as much as I thought, but the wind, if faint, is favorable. She's slipping through the water very nicely. It's too bad she's leaking, but I can assure you we'll beat the *Flying Cloud* record by several hours, pilot to pilot at least.

He has said this from the break of the poop and the statement is greeted by loud cheers from the gold-seekers.

WARREN

I want to give you a watch in commemoration of making this record.

ETHAN

I'll be giving up the sea, now that I've beaten her. I've been talking to the sea as much as to you.

Suddenly the wind dies down and gradually peters out completely. A moment of dead silence, then the chanty, then a wail from members of the crew and the gold-seekers, "The wind is dead."

Damn!

NANCY

Flies into his arms, terrified.

Ethan! The wind is dying!

ETHAN

No, after what we did, she can't do that to us.

He commands.

Send the wind, I say!

The wind comes.

You see.

He speaks to all of them.

It was only a streak of calm, not unusual—make it blow stronger from now in. I'd put more sail on her but every sail is set now. But don't worry, we will get to Golden Gate faster than any man has travelled by sea before.

He goes back into the wheelhouse.

NANCY
Comes forward, now reassured.
For a moment I was frightened.

DICKEY
For a moment I doubted God.

SARA
It's funny, I was looking at Nancy and Ethan together and I felt a chill of horror run down my spine.

Nancy touches Sara as she passes. Sara shrinks.

NANCY
What's the matter? Is my touch—?

SARA
No, no. I was just startled.

NANCY
For a moment in Ethan's arms then I felt so guilty. It was absurd.

SARA
Of course, dear! Why in the world would you feel guilty? You are lovers and love is worth all it costs!

NANCY
Of course!

Curtain

ACT FOUR, SCENE TWO

Scene   *The same, some hours later, sunset. A dead
calm.*

*The clanking of the pump is louder and quicker
now, the chanty is a more powerful groundswell, while the gold-seekers' song is beaten and
exhausted, with only occasional bursts of desperate assertion. The same groups as before are
disclosed on deck. Their mood is even more
strained than in the previous scene.*

WARREN

There's still some hope that the wind will start up again in
time to save the record.

NANCY

Yes, Ethan will drive us through.

WARREN
Thinks.

And yet I wonder if this calm isn't the punishment for Ethan's
crime and Nancy's and Leda's lust.

NANCY

I'm sure the ship must be moving a little and has been moving.
Our watches must be wrong, we've been in this calm only a
short time. There's still hope.

WARREN
To Dickey.

Pray, you fool, you! What are you for, anyway? What do we
support you for? Pray for success for us and see that we get
it or else we'll find a way to get on without you!

DICKEY

There's no use praying. This is God's punishment for the crime
and lust on this ship—the gambling.

WARREN

How about your own lust—the worst of all? We're only human, but you're not supposed to be.

DICKEY

Yes, that's true. We must all repent before it's too late.
Calls on them.
I'm the greatest sinner in the world but the blood of the Lamb will still wash me clean.

ALL *(except Jonathan)*

Yes, we've sinned.
They sing a hymn and all except Jonathan bow their heads.

JONATHAN

I told you so. This all comes of dead, old-fashioned sail, at the mercy of the sea. With steamers, machines, men won't be dependent on Nature—the sea. They will conquer it.

SARA

Maybe it's partly my fault for not remembering the religion of my sainted mother. Bless me—

JONATHAN

Now watch out, Mother. That's the touch of the poet in you coming out.

SARA
Indignantly.

Nonsense!

JONATHAN

Just keep your head clear, you'll need it on land tomorrow. Forget the record, it doesn't matter. Steamers will smash any sail record to bits within a few years anyway. I'm sorry for Ethan, but it's his own fool fault for chasing rainbows.

WARREN

Yes, the sin was all the fault of the ship, in a way. It's made my daughter act like a dirty little slut.

ELIZABETH

A fine example you set, you old whoremonger!

WARREN

I curse the day you were born to disgrace me!

ELIZABETH

And I the day I was born of such a father!

DICKEY

You should be ashamed.

ELIZABETH

You have no reason to be proud yourself!
She shrinks from Jonathan.
You beast!

JONATHAN

I? As I remember, it was you—
Then, calmly.
Keep your head. This will all be good for you, teach you to be a helping brain instead of a sexual organ—the kind of wife I want who will be an asset, a partner—not the animal that I can always buy—from Leda's kind.

ELIZABETH

It's a lie! It's you who were the animal. I was a pure girl. I never dreamed—I never let myself dream—

NANCY

In a daze of love.
Poor Ethan!

ELIZABETH

Viciously.
How about the poor old man who was your husband? Murderer!

NANCY

Turns to Sara.
Don't let her say such things, Mrs. Harford!

SARA

But it's your fault, for leading Ethan to crime. No, I'll be just.

Aside.
You would have told me to be just, Simon.
Then, to Nancy.
No, what Ethan did, he did of his own will.

NANCY

But he didn't, he didn't! He is innocent. I alone am to blame.
She goes to the wheelhouse and as she passes, each calls after her, "Murderer!"

JONATHAN

Yes, it was your fault, Nancy. And it'll be a great handicap for me to make a start here under the cloud of Ethan's disgrace.

DICKEY

There'll still be a chance for our making the record if we cleanse the ship of sin by sacrificing the sinners to the sea—to God. Throw them overboard!

They all rush forward. ETHAN *comes out of the cabin with* NANCY *in the red light of sunset. A howl of execration rises from the crew and the gold-seekers.*

WARREN

Wait. I want to announce something. Maybe we have beaten the record after all!

Ethan draws a pistol. HONEY *has come out of the wheelhouse.*

HONEY

Put that popgun away! It's a waste of powder to shoot fools.
He rushes to the break of the poop.
Wait, boys. As you see, I'm drunk again.
Laughter.

DICKEY

Drunkenness is sinful.

HONEY

Oh, shut up!

108

The crowd jeers.

Why should we get excited about the record, about sin! Ain't we all sinners and proud of it? We'll all be ashore tomorrow, anyway. There's gold waiting for you. To hell with this old tub! You couldn't go gold-seeking tonight in the dark, anyway. But see, there's the land, the Golden Gate, and behind it are the hills full of gold. I promise you you'll all be rich—and you know me, Honey Harford. My word is as good as my bond. And now you've still plenty of whiskey, why not celebrate the end of this damned voyage? And you can ask me to have a drink with you and maybe I will. And I promise you I'll see that you get everything your heart desires tomorrow.

He goes down to them. They go off forward.

DICKEY

Of course, he's right. It's silly to quarrel with the will of God. He is simply showing us the futility of our little vanities. Making a record wouldn't have saved any souls, would it? It was a very successful meeting, though. I was in good voice. I had them in the hollow of my hand—should have passed the plate. But after all it's better to leave vengeance to the Lord, and the sinner's conscience. It relieves one of responsibility.

WARREN

I'm eager to get the ship sold. She's wracked to pieces. I wish she would sink, then I'd have the insurance. You're quite right, Jonathan, sail is dead. Steam is the future. Let's drink, forget the voyage. I'm afraid we none of us were ourselves. That fool Ethan! Records are good for business but a record for a dead issue! And yet he gets us all worked up over it! As for the crime we think Nancy and Ethan committed, there's no proof, and it's the business of the police, not ours. We don't want to be involved as witnesses. I'll fire Ethan though. I wouldn't sleep with a good conscience if I didn't, and he's unfitted for a job in the new age, anyway.

Calls to Ethan coldly.

I hereby fire you, Captain, because of your negligence, your disregard for my property, and the safety of the passengers, your failure to win the record when it was within your grasp.

ETHAN

Very good, sir. There's a breeze springing up now, if you'll notice. We should sight land soon and be at the Golden Gate by midnight, although we'll have to wait for the pilot in the morning.

He goes into the wheelhouse.

NANCY

Ethan!

She follows him in.

DICKEY

Then we weren't in sight of land. I could have sworn I saw—

WARREN

Laughs.

That Honey! He'll wind up in the Senate, if he doesn't look out!

Curtain*

---

* O'Neill's second thoughts (from the scenario):
Sara not in scene—has gone to stateroom—couldn't bear face it(?)—
Eliz. out of scene after talk to Nancy—goes below to avoid her(?)
Or scene ends with Honey's speech (?)
Or Ethan goes back in wheelhouse after his announcement (?)

ACT FOUR, SCENE THREE

Scene   *From astern looking forward as in Scene Three*
of Act Three. It is midnight. Moonlight shines
through the fog. A gentle breeze comes from
astern. The interiors are shown of the wheel-
house, Sara's stateroom, the Captain's stateroom,
the after-cabin. In the wheelhouse, GRABER *and*
WOLFE *are playing cards,* LEDA *sitting beside*
Graber as if it were she who is playing against
Wolfe; HONEY *and* JONATHAN *are looking on,*
ETHAN *is standing in the starboard doorway*
staring out into the fog; SARA *is in her state-*
room; ELIZABETH *is by the rail to the left of the*
wheelhouse.

In the wheelhouse.

GRABER

Well, I've lost.

LEDA

Let's make it short. We'll triple the stakes.

JONATHAN

Don't do it, Wolfe. You're way ahead. It's all to Graber's
advantage.

WOLFE
Stares at him coldly.
Your values are nothing to me.
To Leda.
I accept your bet.

JONATHAN

You fool!
He turns away and talks to Honey.
Crazy fools, both of them! One happy if he loses, the other
indifferent to winning. It's mad. You should play the game
to win.

111

HONEY

Sshh! Ethan will hear you. My own philosophy is that gambling is silly unless you run the house and let the suckers give you their money.

To the left of the wheelhouse.

ELIZABETH
Thinks.

It's just a business proposition with Jonathan. I can't forget the joy of my shame when Father called me a dirty little trollop. But did Jonathan ever love me, even want me instead of just a woman? I must know.
Calls to him.

Oh, Jonathan!

HONEY
Your lady love is calling.

JONATHAN
Goes out to her.

You'll be catching cold, Elizabeth. You ought to go to bed.

ELIZABETH
Encouraged.

Don't pretend. You don't really love me, do you?

JONATHAN
Don't let's get sentimental.

ELIZABETH
You didn't even want me.

JONATHAN
A man always wants a woman.

ELIZABETH
A woman, yes, but not me particularly, did you? You only did it so that I'd have to marry you, and because you thought it was what I wanted.

JONATHAN
Yes, that's true.

112

ELIZABETH

For my money?

JONATHAN

No, I'll make my own money, but to get an opening wedge, yes. But that wasn't all. I'd studied you. Except for your craziness on this voyage, you are intelligent, you'll make a good wife, and I'll make a good husband. I won't run after other women.

ELIZABETH

Because you don't care.

JONATHAN

I'll give you power and money. I'll be in your debt at first but I'll pay it back a hundredfold. It will be a partnership.

ELIZABETH

Coldly.

Yes, I suppose so.

JONATHAN

I think we ought to get married tonight. So long as it happens during the trip, no one will question exactly when.

ELIZABETH

Yes. I feel like a dirty little slut who has sold herself for counterfeit.

JONATHAN

Marriage will cure that.

WARREN

Comes up.

I'd like to speak to my daughter for a moment.

Jonathan moves off.

It's hard for a father to speak with his daughter, but are you sure?

ELIZABETH

Yes, and we've just been talking. We've decided to get married at once.

WARREN

Yes, perhaps that is best. Dickey is still awake. I heard him praying in his stateroom. Well, I'll be sorry to lose you, Elizabeth.

ELIZABETH

Rot! Don't introduce sentiment. You'll be glad to get rid of me and I'll be glad to get away from you. I gave myself to Jonathan deliberately. I wanted a husband. He's got brains, ability, he'll make good. You'll give him a good opening. He doesn't want any money.

WARREN

Yes, it's better than I thought. And if he doesn't make good, you can always divorce him.

ELIZABETH

Exactly.

WARREN

Well, it might be worse. I'll go and arrange matters with Dickey and then call up for you.
He goes.

ELIZABETH
Laughs bitterly.
What am I hurt about? After all, I always swore I'd be loved for my brain and not my body. I've got what I wanted.

In the wheelhouse, JONATHAN *has come back.*

GRABER

I've lost again.

LEDA

We'll double the stakes again.

The sound of eight bells. JACKSON, *the first mate, comes up to relieve the watch.* ETHAN *seems oblivious.*

JONATHAN

Why don't you go to bed, Ethan?

Ethan gives orders and goes out on deck. He seems to be speaking to the sea.

HONEY
To Jonathan.
He's strange. We'd better watch him.

They go out.

JONATHAN
Don't be so upset, Ethan. You're a good loser and, in the long run, this will be a good thing. It will get you off the sea—a dead issue.

ETHAN
You mean well, Jonathan, but your values are not mine. The sea is a symbol of life to me.
Then sharply.
I murdered the first mate, I murdered the Captain, in order that I might possess life.

HONEY
Glory be to God, don't say that!

ETHAN
It's true.

JONATHAN
You're a fool. You shouldn't trust even us with such a secret!

ETHAN
You'll be a great success in the world, Jonathan, but a horrible failure in life—and you may not ever realize it.

JONATHAN
I'll take care of *my* life. It's *your* life—

ETHAN
I'll take care of that.

JONATHAN
I think you're playing the romantic Harford—covering up for Nancy.

115

ETHAN

I killed them.

JONATHAN

Well, no one suspects—no one can prove—

ETHAN

I know.

JONATHAN

You're not going to confess, are you? You've got to consider the family, our name. It's going to be hard enough to get started out here on a shoestring without—

ETHAN

I said you'd be a great success. No, I'm not going to confess.

JONATHAN

Good. I don't believe you anyway. It isn't possible.

ETHAN

And now that's off your conscience.

JONATHAN

Go to bed—get some sleep.

> *Warren calls Elizabeth. She calls Jonathan.*
> *They go off rear.*

HONEY

Breaks down.

Good God, Ethan, how could you? But I'm not blaming you. I'll stick by you. To hell with them all! We Harfords'll beat the devil if we stick together.

ETHAN

Pats Honey on the back.

Thanks, Honey. I'm afraid I've felt a superior contempt for you. Forgive it.

HONEY

Nothing. Sure, I'm nothing much.

116

ETHAN

Go down to Mother. I know that she knows, that she's grieving alone. I can't go to her yet, not until I can bring her a
decision she'll approve.

HONEY

I'll go, but hadn't you better go to Nancy? She's alone too.

ETHAN

I have to bring her a decision, too.
Then, suddenly.
I'm glad this has all happened. I'm glad I staked everything,
committed crimes to win. I'm glad I lost. If it were only myself
I would know what to do and do it this instant. I'd let the sea
possess what it has won and, beyond desire for possession, I
might find peace at last.

HONEY

You mean you—? Don't!
He grabs Ethan's arm.

ETHAN

I said I hadn't come to a decision—what to do with love. Go
to Mother.

Honey goes.

In the cabin below, NANCY *comes from her stateroom into Ethan's.*

NANCY

The watch has changed. Why doesn't he come? I seem to see
Enoch lying there. It was a terrible crime, yet I can't seem to
pray. I don't care, Ethan loves me, that's all that matters.
She runs from the room.

The scene switches to ETHAN *standing above.*

ETHAN

I've got to go down and face her. But I don't really love her,
it was only the lust to possess. If I could only go down and say
I love you. But I can't face that horror of stricken loneliness
in her eyes. To kill a body, what is that? But I can't murder a

soul. And how can one lie to a soul? I can't go to her. Maybe
I should just jump overboard? No, Sea, you can't have such a
complete victory as that. I will never surrender unconditionally.

> *He goes into the wheelhouse to avoid temptation.*

WOLFE

I thought you wouldn't go without saying good-bye.

ETHAN

I won't, Wolfe.

LEDA
Unnerved.

For Christ's sake, aren't you human at all?

WOLFE

Hardly at all, I hope. Humane, rather. My line?

> *The scene switches to Sara's room.* HONEY *enters.*

SARA

I was feeling desperate and uneasy. I'm glad you came, but
where's Ethan?

HONEY

On deck. He's all right. And Wolfe keeps on winning. He has
the devil's own luck—he's a born gambler. Why don't you get
him to start a gambling house? He doesn't care what he does,
and he'll do anything you ask.

SARA

Yes, my father was a great gambler, but of course he always
lost. It would be only right for Wolfe to win it back. But that's
a terrible thing for you and me to be thinking. Why doesn't
Ethan come down?

HONEY

He says he'll be coming down to you soon, but he's got to decide something first.

SARA
Terrified.

Glory be to God!

HONEY

What's the matter? It's only as to whether he'll leave the sea or not.

SARA

No—your father would always come to me when—and he'd leave it to my honor. God damn the Harfords—their honor—it's like a devil they cast from themselves to you to possess you with.
Pause.
Oh, Honey, I'm terrified the Captain didn't die—

HONEY
Tries to comfort her.
Now, Mother, don't be imagining such nonsense!

SARA

Yes, of course it's nonsense.

The scene switches to the Captain's cabin.

NANCY
Enters again.
I can't stand it—I've got to see him.
Calls up stairs.
Oh, Ethan!

Above, he starts, but pretends not to hear.

LEDA

Nancy's calling you, Ethan. She's alone. She's afraid. I can tell by her voice. Aren't you going down?
As he hesitates.
For Christ's sake, aren't *you* human either?

ETHAN

I'm going.

LEDA

No, maybe you'd better stay—No, what good would that do?
Turns to Graber.
Triple stakes this time, Ben. We'll beat him yet.

119

Ethan goes down.

NANCY

Come into my room, where we've loved, where we can forget.

ETHAN

No, let's stay here and face it.

NANCY

I'll face anything with you, even hell. Hell with you will be heaven, if you only love me.

ETHAN

Lies.

Of course I love you, and there'll be no hell for us—only the sea. We'll sleep in each other's arms.

> *He kisses her, but she senses it is only desire, that he remains himself, he still possesses himself.*

NANCY

Besides the guilt is all mine. You merely struck the first mate, you didn't kill him. He did that when he fell and fractured his skull. And it was I who killed the Captain. I took the pillow from your hands. No, Ethan, I've decided that I must confess, take all the blame, and set you free.

ETHAN

Probing her cruelly.

You mean you want me to be free to marry some other woman, to have children by her, happiness with her? You'd absolutely give me up in your head and heart and then still go on, when I don't love you?

NANCY

Yes, I'd still go on even then because I love you.

ETHAN

Breaking.

Oh, Nancy! Do you think I could accept that? I also have my pride. No, we will go together.

NANCY

Oh, Ethan, you do love me then. I'm so glad.

ETHAN

Excuse me for a moment. I must talk to Mother.
He goes to his mother's cabin.
Honey, I want to talk with Mother alone.
Honey goes.
I've decided what I must do, Mother. Nancy has just shown me
by being willing to face everything, alone, without fear. You
must see that this is the best. I'll make Nancy think I really
do love her.

The scene switches briefly to Nancy's cabin.

NANCY

I can face all my crimes, proudly, without fear. Hell together
with Ethan *will* be heaven!

The scene returns to SARA *and* ETHAN.

SARA

Oh, Ethan, please! I want to help you, but you can't ask me
to agree to this, my own son!

ETHAN

You love me!

SARA

Of course I do, but I also remember you as a baby. Have
mercy!

ETHAN

No, you must judge me, Mother.

SARA

Oh, go away! Don't tell me about it, do as you please.

ETHAN
Starts to go.
All right, but I thought you would never forgive me if I
didn't—

SARA

And you're right—I never would. Now go, and God damn the honor of the Harfords!

Ethan goes. HONEY *comes back.*

Get me drunk, Honey. I'll get drunk. I'll be a drunken peasant woman from this out. I'll tell the honor of the Harfords and the honor of my lying, drunken sponge of a father to kiss my arse!

HONEY

Comforts her, offers her a drink.

Yes, a drink will do you good, Mother.

SARA

Dashes the drink from his hand.

And I a sodden coward like my father, drunk, afraid of life! I'll face it, I say—I'll face it with honor, like your father faced it, God rest his soul!

She collapses, weeping.

The scene switches to the Captain's room. ETHAN *takes* NANCY's hand.

NANCY

Up those stairs?

ETHAN

Yes, that must be the way.

They go up. As they appear at the head of the stairs, the card game stops.

Good-bye, Wolfe—and to Honey when you see him.

WOLFE

Good-bye, Ethan. I understand.

LEDA

Starts up.

Wait! You can't—No! What the hell am I saying? Go on! Get out of here! God bless you!

Nancy and Ethan go out, hand in hand.

ETHAN

We'll swim out together—until the fog lifts. And then the sea will be alight with beauty forevermore—because you are you.

They disappear off rear in the fog.

GRABER

I've lost everything. Oh, thank God, thank God, every cent I stole for you, Leda. I've lost it all! I'm free!

LEDA

You're not rid of your conscience yet. Play him for *me*—all he's won against *me*!

GRABER

No!

LEDA

Then *I'll* play him. Here.

WOLFE

Agitatedly.

No, I don't want you.

LEDA

Have you been playing for what you want? Then you're a fake —or else you're afraid of yourself.

WOLFE

I'll play.

LEDA

No, cut! Quick! Mine's a ten! Cut, coward! Let me see. The queen of hearts! My God, he's won me with the queen of hearts!

WOLFE

I'll give you back to Graber.

GRABER

No, I don't want her now. I can be boss now, I'm free.

LEDA

To Wolfe.

You think you can get rid of me, do you? Oh, no, Wolfe. Never! I love you, you fool—can't you see I love you?*

The scene switches to Sara's cabin.

SARA

She senses the moment Ethan and Nancy go overboard from the bow and leaps to her feet.

Ethan! My first-born!

Curtain

Casa Genotta, June 9, 1935

---

* O'Neill's notes for the revision of the play include an expanded version of this scene.

THE SCENARIO

"A TOUCH OF THE POET"

from starboard as in 3—2, but no interiors are revealed

Scene Two—The same, some hours later, sunset

Scene Three—The same as 3—3, midnight of same day

? Epilogue—

CHARACTERS

Simon Harford
Sara, his wife
Ethan, First mate, clipper ship "Dream Of The West"
Wolfe, clerk in a bank
Jonathan, clerk railroad office
Honey, tin peddler
Captain Enoch Payne
Theodore [*added above:* Lester] Warren, owner
Elizabeth, his daughter
Ben Graber
Leda* Cade
Jackson, 1st mate
Rev. Samuel Dickey
Nancy Drummond (Mrs Enoch Payne)

* Written in over an erasure. Earlier names considered were first Goldie
and then Lisa, both of which occur in the scenario.—*Ed.*

"THE CALMS OF CAPRICORN"

ACT ONE—SCENE ONE

Scene—The same as Epilogue of "More Stately Mansions",
the potato field on Sara's farm. It is now the spring of 1857,
a fine morning. Cato, a middle-aged negro, a fugitive slave, is
discovered. He is lazily making motions of work with a hoe,
singing mournfully, grumbling aloud to himself. He is disil-
lusioned with freedom—same old work—no freedom from that
—he earns a few dollars a month but since he spends it on
drink and gambling and is broke next day, what good is it?—
He laments the good old days in Georgia, the food, the quarters, the merriment, the climate as contrasted with N[ew].
E[ngland].—the "quality folks" who owned him compared to
the Harfords—Simon, they say was "quality" but he certainly
isn't now. Of the children only Wolfe is his idea of gentleman
—comes from mixture—as he overheard his old master say,
the Irish trash coming in are ruining the country—but here he
shows he likes Sara in spite of her no caste—but she expects
him to work too hard—ten men's work—sees her coming—
scared—begins working hard and lamenting—why did he ever
let those fools persuade him to run off with them—and why
when he was finally caught in Mass. did Simon have to interfere
and buy his freedom—Simon the most interfering man—he
chuckles, old master skinned him on deal, 1000 for me while in
Geo[rgia]. I'd be dear at 500—thus illogically pride and respect
for Simon for seeing his true value.

Sara comes in—amused and exasperated—"give me that
hoe"—he resists, scandalized—lectures her, supposing any of
the white folks should see her—begins to work frantically, will
kill himself working rather than have her guilty of such a social
outrage—for his sake as well as hers, he doesn't want people
saying he belongs to a family whose Misses [*i.e.*, Missus] works
in fields like a hand—then he looks toward farm—"what I tell
you? White folks calling—they see you here—coming up—

131

supposin' I'd let you take the hoe?" "It's Capt. Payne & his wife. They know I've worked in fields and never thought less of me" "Can't be quality, then. And you ain't worked since I came. Massa Harford he told me see you don't, and I've done it"

Captain Payne & Nancy come in—greetings—Cato says more weeds down yonder and runs off—Sara expresses surprise, didn't expect ship in so soon—Payne says made fine passage—good winds from Line up—and with sensible sailing, not cracking on like maniacs, and ruining good ship to get name in papers—"I suppose I'm an old-fashioned sea-dog—love ship" (then laughing but with resentment) "your son, Ethan, would tell you what an old fogey he thinks me—craze for speed—make a record if you wreck ship", etc.—Sara asks "How is Ethan?" "Fine" "Is he coming home to visit? [*Added above:* I hoped he would, I wrote him father had been ill]—didn't last two trips—wrote he would have too much work on board. Payne smiles, well, that's hardly true, But Ethan is young, you mustn't mind. I suppose the real reason is that he's some girl in N.Y.—Nancy "Oh, no, I'm sure it's not that"—Sara looks at her—[*added above:* then casual talk of panic, hard times]—Payne takes leave—driving on—call for wife on his return.

Sara begins slyly pumping Nancy, isn't she getting tired of life on ship—"I couldn't stand it", fear of sea, memories of her crossing and seasickness—Nancy says no, ship has become like home now, you know reason I went, when child died 5 years ago, the sea wipes out memory—then Sara gets her to talking of Ethan—she is embarrassed, then blurts out wanted to speak about him, tell Sara to persuade him to change to another ship, needs change, his chance—"I have studied Ethan—of course, don't pretend to understand him, he never confides, or hardly ever talks, etc.—but I am sure he feels thwarted, no chance get on, queer struggle always going on underneath with husband—she makes comparisons which unconsciously make dry old figure of husband, romantic figure of Ethan—he is so proud, so fierce, he was born to command, etc.—and husband old friend of owner, also very healthy in spite of age and so will never retire—also 1st mate always sailed with him, no chance there—Sara looks at her "Then you think I ought to try and

get him to go on other ship?" "Yes, I think that would be best"
"Well, there's only one way I ever discovered to get Ethan to
do what you want and that's to advise him to do what you
don't want and he'll be sure to act the opposite" "Yes, he has
a fierce pride in preserving his independence, in not letting any
one or anything get any hold on him, I feel that. That's why
he hates the sea, because he loves it" then apologizes again
"But you must think it funny to have me discussing him so
intimately. Why, really, I hardly know him. He's so reserved,
so silent—and so entirely different from other men, you feel—
so sensitive under his hard reserve—and so isolated and lonely
in his freedom, etc." "Yes, he's a touch of the poet in him, God
pity him, like his father" "Oh, but it's wonderful to have that
touch of the poet in you, don't you think? Yes, Ethan is a poet.
I've felt that." "Well, I'll do my best to get him out of your
ship. I agree with you now that would be best" Frightened,
Nancy reverses "Ah, but don't take my word for it. I really
shouldn't have spoken. I may be quite wrong, etc.—and, of
course, Capt. Payne would hate losing such a fine officer, really
fond of him underneath, I'm sure my husband would be very
angry if he knew I had spoken—so you must use own judgment." "I will" Nancy changes subject "How is your husband?"
Sara answers Oh, never better, [*added above:* almost recovered
from illness] he has new interest in life since he's been going
with Honey on tin wagon—"then he isn't working on book"—
Sara laughs "No. He's taking a vacation from that. He'll never
finish it, I'm thinking. He's all the time finding more he wants
to put in it. It'll be in fifty volumes if he ever does finish it. But
it keeps him occupied and not trying to help me on the farm.
He was never cut out for a farmer"—sees rig drawing up to
house—it's Ethan—Nancy in embarrassed flurry to get away
but doesn't know how—Sara waves—Ethan comes—greets
Nancy with formal polite indifference—she makes excuses,
knows they want to be alone, will meet husband on road, wants
to walk, etc.—she goes.

Sara, to test Ethan, remarks how pretty Nancy is—he replies indifferently "Is she? I suppose she is. I've never noticed.
Just the wife of that old fool to me". "He was here a while
ago. He was saying the reason you hadn't come home your last

two voyages was you'd probably some girl you were after in New York" "He would think that" "It isn't true, then? It would be only natural" "No, it isn't true. I have no interest in women" (then bluntly) "The reason I didn't come home, if you must know, is that I was ashamed of always turning up the same old 2nd mate. But here I am. I wasn't coming this time either—but, somehow, I suddenly felt lonely & homesick —a bit sick of the sea & its disappointments—and your letter about father had made me anxious [*Opposite:* Change to, had written him about father's illness]—you wrote at such great length and said so much without really saying anything— you're not a very skilful liar, Mother—I take after you in that —but you succeeded in making me very curious. Perhaps that's what you wanted. Well, now I'm here tell me what's happened —She goes back—you know how he has lived in books ever since we came out here, and in the writing of his own book, going to his shack by the sea every morning to work—and want- ing to help me on the farm in the afternoons only I'd never let him—"You were wrong—made him ashamed" "I couldn't see him do it. He's gentleman—and besides I'd always a feeling he didn't want me to let him help" "And yet he did want, I know. What was the last title of book?" "The Meaning Of Life" "Ah! No wonder he can't finish it!" "He's given it up. He's destroyed it. He came to me one day and told me it was all a fake. Most of the days he's gone to the shack he'd never written a line but just sat and dreamed and stared at sea. He cried. He said he'd been just a sponging loafer and a faker. But he'd done with dreams and a barren solitude. There was still time to live— Open Road—quoted—and then what do you think?—He said he'd go out on the wagon with Honey tin-peddling, and since he's done that he's a changed man, and full of gossip and the news of the world and politics—but there's something forced about it as if he was driving himself"—"Forward to belonging? I know. But we Harfords are aliens now. We can never belong" [*Opposite:* His scorn for father—always wanted this & that, too—but you can't have both—must give this for that—should have gone & lived alone—turned his back on family—or should never have married—has always remained child, first tied to mother's apron strings, then to yours—Sara takes this half-indignantly, half-comically—] "It's been a great sorrow to me, his going. I thought if I lived here simple on the land as he'd always said he wanted, he'd be happy at last" "You thought he knew what he wanted. But we Harfords don't. We only pursue a [*added above:* mysterious] great need behind all wants, of which the wants are delusive shadows" "You sound unhappy" "I? No—only suffering from blind alley sickness. Been static too long. But if the wall doesn't move out of my way soon, I'll find some way to move it" (he forces smile) "In plain words, I've been second officer too long. I'm getting nowhere" "Then why not change ship?" "No, can't explain feeling, but it must be this ship and no other—it is this because of my fate—it is the test, the particular challenge of the sea to me. I feel if I were to exchange & become captain in a day, it would be failure and cowardice—and how the sea would laugh in derision!" [*Opposite:* He explains bitter dissatisfaction with present life—sea meant freedom from all land values—but he finds himself enslaved by them—always obeying orders—also feels love for sea & hates it for it—wants to break away—his idea to experience all the freedom of the spirit—would go on to conquest of high mountains, tear their gold from them as gesture of conquest—Sara interested materialistically, questions as to Cal[ifornia]., Jonathan wants to go, why hasn't he left ship, gone to mines?—Ethan scornful & insulted then laughs—can't leave sea unless he has conquered it first, leave sea freed by own choice as commander, not beaten by it—] She starts talking practicalities, captain to partnership, ownership, freedom" He laughs "Mother Possessions! Your freedom on this earth, this field, is that it belongs to you etc. but to me to be earthbound by possessions is slavery. What can it profit a man if he own the world and pay his soul for it? But I can see that for a woman the reverse is true, what could her soul profit her if she paid the earth for it?" "I don't understand. What is it you want, Ethan" "I want nothing. It is what I need that I must have —must & will have—and will gladly pay the world for" "And what's that?" "Victory over the sea—and so, freedom & re-birth" "I don't understand" "Not with your head—but with

135

your heart, you guess—for I know you love me, Mother" "I do" "And I speak to you in symbols which neither of us can think but which our hearts understand, because I love you, and because I love and hate the sea, which you can understand, being also a mother. For the sea is the mother of life—is a woman of all moods for all men—and all seductive & evil—devil mother or wife or mistress or daughter or water-front drab—and it is as a sign and symbol of freedom to me that someday as captain of a ship I shall fight her storms and calms and fogs and cross-currents and capricious airs and make a faster voyage around the Horn to the Golden Gate than ever man has made—as a last gesture of victory, now when the era of American triumph over sea is dying from this money panic of the greedy earthbound. And if I smash the ship to pieces under me in the victory, well, one always pays for victory with one's temporal life that the soul may win freedom. I want this chance to accept the sea's challenge, that's all. If I win, I possess her and she cringes and I kick her away from me and turn my back forever. If I lose, I give myself to her as her conquest and she swallows and spews me out in death." (he looks at her troubled sad face & laughs) "But what has all this to do with freight rates and ship-building, etc., you're wondering. And the answer to that is easy. Nothing, nothing at all. (he laughs) Poor mother. It must be a bitter blow to you to have such a mad offspring" [*Opposite:* Sara in brogue angrily bawls out Abigail [*i.e.*, Deborah Harford] (he mentions or quotes her)—it's that old mad lunatic puts such thoughts in head—trying to ruin you as she did father—Ethan arrogantly denies anyone can influence him—I am my own!—no woman's—] "Poor Nancy" "Eh? What?" "Nothing. You say you love me—" "And I do, don't doubt that. And I love father—or perhaps I only pity him because I understand him. And I like Honey—and dislike Jonathan—and respect Wolfe because he respects nothing." "No, you don't even love yourself" "Ah, that's the point. I seek to so live that I may at the last at least come to a true self-respect that would be a reason for love." (he laughs) "Poor mother, I say again. How I have unburdened myself to you. That's why I really came here, I see now—for

I feel unloaded, freer, ready for a new voyage. But you look puzzled and sad. (He pats her hand) "Never mind. The brain is a latecomer. It knows nothing yet of life before it came. But the heart is old as life. It understands, eh, mother?" (She smiles and kisses him—in brogue) "It does, devil take it. It understands it's a hard fate for a woman to have been the daughter & wife & mother of men touched with the curse of the poet. For it's the moon you want and you hunt her in the skies of the broad day when the rest of us don't see her there at all."— (Sees Honey & Harford coming out of house—alarm—can't yawp at Honey—goes off—Ethan starts to follow her, then stops—Simon, Sara & Honey come in)—Sara expostulating with Simon, bawling out Honey—"but he insisted. I couldn't hold him down, and I thought a bit of sun & fresh air"—Simon agrees—sends Honey to Cato—turns to Ethan & Sara feels they want to be alone—goes to farmhouse to see about cooking—from end of field comes Honey's voice singing "The praties they grow small"—both are silent, listening—Simon says "do you know last verse?"—recites words—(he repeats words first verse(?))—then silence again—Simon "You & I have been always strangers to each other, such strangers that I know there is a soul so identical in each that we have never felt the need to be anything but strangers." [*Opposite:* Change this scene to Simon talking, Ethan humoring him with a sort of affectionate disdainful condescension—until father speaks of sea as she—

Or strange scene between them in which each talks about other but neither pays any attention to what other says until sea comes up] "Yes, I have guessed that, Father" "There is no Father between us. Call me brother—or simply, man"—then he goes on to say strangely, you will understand if I speak to you, after our lifelong silence, in words that would seem strange to those whose spirit has no ears. But I awoke just now from a dream of unity—a premonition and a prophecy, too, I think—" E[than]. catches this, glances at him understandingly "Yes, I think so. But let that be a secret between us." He goes on "The peace of that dream is still on me, and the intuition. In the dream the opposites at last blended and were one, and even now as the dream recedes, I am still in a place where the edges of the opposites still merge, and I can see and guess so much that is behind the senses. And I speak to the part of me which is three parts of you, and therefore is the dominant you, the you which is a fierce contempt for men and for yourself, a fierce pride and a lust for power & possession—but in the spirit, not the flesh. Can you hear me, man?" "I hear you" "I have only this to say. For you life is the sea. You think you will force your will on her and make her yours, and thereby dictate the terms by which she may possess you?" "Right or wrong, it is the only way I can achieve meaning in my own eyes, expiate being myself, be able to forgive myself, be able to go on with pride. Right or wrong, it is my meaning." (defiantly) "You do not think I can win? But I will win! Nothing shall stand in the way of my winning! Nothing! I will be as unscrupulous as the sea" "I think you will lose, that if you win, you will have lost most of all. But I also know that your losing will be your final victory and release. But do not think I am presuming to advise you, or disapprove. On the contrary, you are doing the only thing that man, a lonely exile in a world of matter, can do—to choose his dream and then to follow that dream to the end," etc.

Sara comes back—worried, wants Simon go in—but he insists on staying—Ethan goes off see Honey—then scene of Simon's strange hail & farewell to Sara—still on the plane where the edges of his opposites merge—his reaching out to her over the gulf of their two solitudes—his yearning love & regret for nature, love, the beauty of life—a hymn—his contempt for all reasons, explanations for living, all flights—alike for his search for wisdom and her hunt for material possessions —what is life worth?—and the answer is so simple—life is worth one's life, give life for life—Oh to give oneself to life & love & beauty—to belong—to let oneself be possessed in order to possess—to love and be free, to be freed by love, etc. —I love life, Sara—now, at the last, I love life and I love you, etc.—in this high noon, earth & spirit & you & I are one!—he hugs her to him—then she says anxiously, you are chilled, shivering—he smiles, an old reaction of habit—I have always

been chilled by the hot sun of high noon, I have always shuddered with cold [*added above:* so fatal chill] in the arms of
happiness—but no more—now I shall find even the arms of
night warm—then he quotes the Open Road—she says, come
to house, by the fire—no, no, I am warmed in the warmth of
your heart, Sara Beloved, warmed forevermore—she clasps
him fiercely to her—

Curtain

Scene—Sitting room of the farmhouse, two weeks later—
Simon has died of pneumonia two days before—the four sons
are discovered, waiting for the undertaker and hearse to come
for funeral—Sara is with the body in the next room—Jonathan
speaks of plans, for practical reasons folly for mother cling to
farm, needs complete change, her terrible grief—"I know purchaser for farm"—go to Cal[ifornia].—great chance out there
—into mines—they are all stagnating here—asks Ethan's
views—Ethan antagonistic & contemptuous—know nothing of
your money-grubbing values and don't want to know—quarrel
—but Ethan says sea voyage might be good help mother forget
& when she gets to Cal. she can decide [*opposite:* But can we
get mother give up land—her obsession—only if we all urge
her as one—] —Jonathan turns to Wolfe contemptuously—
"And you, I suppose you don't care whether you stay or go"
—Wolfe replies with his quiet enigmatical smile "No, so I am
perfectly willing to go" "And you, Honey?" "Anywhere where
there's gold to be got without working too hard for it, that's
the land for me"—then he is conscience-stricken, no time to
be talking and planning with father lying dead in next room,
though he used to do a lot of talking himself to me on the
wagon about going to Cal. But the way he talked Cal. was
only a fairyland in his mind."—then, as if conscience bothered
them all, they all begin to talk of father—regrets they didn't
get closer to him, help him more—then resentments, thoughts
of mother—their different ideas of father each a self-revelation
—then they speak of his written directions for funeral service—
queer—he meant something for us by them but what only he
will ever know—"get mother, Honey—she'll wear herself out
in there—hasn't hardly spoken, except to him, since he died—
if we could get her to talk, maybe she'd get it out of system
—don't want her to collapse"

Honey brings in Sara—they hold service (undertaker due
soon)—each has a part of poem to read—then Honey a verse

of song to sing—then as finale Sara opens envelope and reads
what Simon has written for her to read—to the effect that she
has done her duty by him, given her own life in love to protect,
comfort and save him but now that he is dead, that life is over
and a new life opens for her, she must not let his memory
stand in way, she must forget him and be free—She reacts to
this with reproachful, despairing tenderness. "Forget you,
Simon? It's little you know of love, God help you!" etc.—and
she takes an oath to remain faithful to his memory—then she
goes on in a sort of [*added above:* sutie [*i.e.,* suttee?]] keen for
the dead, to go back in memory over their whole life together
—Jonathan tries to stop her but Honey tells him let her go on
and say all that is in her heart—and he keeps making responses
to encourage her—she extols all his virtues, a poet, a child,
too good for this world—she reproaches herself, she should
have done more, should have understood him better, should
never have let her greed take him into business, she should
have done all the work and left him free for his high thoughts
of beauty and search for the wisdom of life—blames herself
for ever letting him go back to mother—that brought his loneliness back to him—then laments for the lovely soul in him and
tender reproach—if he'd only given her that soul how she
would have loved and protected it—but then she defends him
—he wanted to but it wasn't in his power, it was a cross laid
on him, a curse he couldn't shake off—then fiercely "And why
am I complaining? Wasn't it a beautiful life I've lived, even
the sorrow in it? How many women have known what I have
known, the feel inside that your heart has borne the man you
love into life, and in your heart he's grown and become a man
and your lover and husband and yet always remained a child,
and at the last his death is only a return behind the gates of
birth to sleep at peace again forever in the love of your heart"
She rises to a pitch of passionate exultance "Yes, I thank
Almighty God for you, Simon, and for the beauty [*added above:*
dream] of the poet's love, and the passion of a man's love,
and the tender dependence of a child's love you brought to me.
And it's the sweet life I've lived with you and I wouldn't change
it if I had a choice of all the lives other women have ever lived
in the world!"

A knock. Jonathan goes out. The undertaker—"only one man with him, we'd better help him"—Sara says wait a minute, final good-bye—Honey says "we'll hold him in the hall till you give the word, Mother"—four go out—Sara has gone to doorway—stops, suddenly feeling awed at how withdrawn he looks, sensitive about intruding on his privacy—he was always such a gentleman, so modest, would never let me see him naked —and now he seems naked to her, so bare and lonely—her tender keen[?]—worried for him, what will he do now without me—then sadly, "but he always was without me, even when he was most with me"—then cries to him desperately in last effort to break down barrier "Simon! this once—only this once —give me all of you for the all of me!"—then sobbing "Forgive me, I have no right to ask it—always thinking of myself— sure, I know you can't—and I'll be happy in your happiness, for don't I know you're happy now—for at last you're free— free even of me—and God bless and preserve you in that freedom". She turns and stumbles blindly to the hall door "Take him now and be quick about it"—She remains there "Free of me—free of me—and you've set me free—I've a new life starting and I'll do as I please now and as I've always wanted and I've four strong sons to work with me and to help me to the wealth and power of this world and all I've dreamed"—all this as if thoughts were running through her mind without her volition—then hammering from next room awakes her and she flies into a frenzy of sorrowful, savage denunciation "Arrah, are those the thoughts you're having now, you shameless creature! May God curse you for a greedy sow and no woman at all!" (then pitifully) "Simon! You didn't hear, did you? And if you heard, sure it's well you must know it's not your love speaking at all! (Hammering from next room)

Curtain

Scene—After cabin of the clipper ship, "Dream Of The West",
at dock in N. Y.—six weeks later—Jonathan & Honey come
out of their stateroom at right—Honey boyishly enthusiastic
and awed by splendid accommodations—Jonathan says all well
enough for sail, but dead, steamers will make it look like
nothing—Rev. Dickey comes out of his room at right—greets
them unctuously, introducing self—"my cabin mate is a Mr.
Harford"—"Our brother"—he goes out—Wolfe comes out of
same cabin—Honey jokes about his bad luck in roommate—
Wolfe smiles indifferently—Jonathan says going out on dock,
look at N. Y.—Honey jokes, don't buy it—"come on"—"no,
I'll wait for mother" [*added above:* Nancy showing her cabin]—
then tries to get Wolfe, who is starting to play solitaire—but
Wolfe indifferent—Jonathan contemptuous, goes out—Sara &
Nancy come out of Nancy's cabin—Sara enthusiastic about her
cabin & captain's—Nancy says "put your mother right next to
us so I can look after her"—Sara asks how long now before
ship sails—Honey teases her, she may well ask, in a stew to
get there hours before [*added above:* Sara tells story how father
nearly missed boat coming over]—Nancy laughingly defends
her, right to avoid last minute crush, although in these hard
times, ship half empty normally—but this voyage, for strange
reason, second cabins forward & steerage(?) full up with a
company of gold-seekers, all from same neighborhood in northern N. Y.—it seems from what Capt. Payne heard, their leader
had heard from brother in Cal[ifornia]. of big new strike and
he'd gotten company together of poor neighbors—it will be
like first days—poor things, I hope they have better luck than
those others, that this wonderful new strike isn't just fairy tale
—Honey impressed, talk with them, get in on it [*opposite:* Introduce scene Ethan & Sara (& Nancy?)—their congrats his
promotion—Sara tells him sure he owes it to Nancy—he is formally thankful—but joking in comical seriousness, says he feels
other woman in it, fate—father told me sea was woman—]—

Nancy speaks [to] Wolfe, doesn't he ever stop playing that game
—He replies with strange, remote pleasant smile, keeps him
from thinking, and hoping and all the rest of it—it's pure art—
without object except itself—no gain—"But don't you ever play
with someone?" "No, that would be to involve myself in the
outside game"—Sara sighs over him helplessly—Honey taunts,
afraid of being beat—Wolfe replies calmly, no, except in so far
as being beaten would imply that the competitive game was
worth winning—Nancy laughs, you're a funny boy, Wolfe—
"Yes, I agree, I know it will sound incredible but I am always
watching myself from inside and laughing—but that I'm laughing at everyone else, too"—Sara, a bit exasperated, "don't mind
his nonsense. He needs a few good hard knocks to wake him
from his dreaming and I'm hoping he'll get them in Cal., or
maybe one or two starters on this voyage." (then smiling) "But
he's a good boy, Nancy, and if his head's full of queer dreams,
it's only the touch of the poet in him he gets from his father,
God rest his soul" Nancy says but surely he's at heart enthusiastic about his brother being appointed 1st mate at last. Wolfe
says smiling without looking up from cards, "I don't know.
Should I be? I would have to be sure first that it is fortunate
to get what one wants" "Oh!" Honey says shrewdly "Is it sure
he's got it. We haven't started yet.—maybe 1st mate will show
up" Nancy says "Oh, no. His doctor told Capt. only this morning his heart was in no condition, he must rest for one voyage
at least, and even a headstrong man like Mr. Hull is bound to
heed that advice. I told the Captain at once he owed it to
Ethan—he rather hesitated, you know he feels Ethan is young
& reckless but I said I'd talk to Ethan and make him behave—
and besides with his mother on board he'd be bound to be on
his best behavior—so Captain gave in." (She laughs joyously)
"Oh, aren't you all glad. Poor Ethan, he's waited so long and
had so many disappointments" (Sara glances at her queerly.
She grows confused) "Oh, I suppose it's wrong of me to rejoice over Mr. Hull's illness but it's really not serious, I believe,
and then I feel toward Ethan as you must feel—like a mother—
and I know how much he wanted this promotion. He was so
excited when he moved things into Mr. Hull's stateroom—like
a boy who's won a prize"—then again catching Sara's eye she

breaks off and changes subject abruptly "But I haven't told you we're to have the owner, Mr. Warren and his only daughter, Elizabeth—he's a widower, she's just 18"—Sara perks up, ah, so the owner & his only daughter—" Honey teases her, "making a match for one of them already [*added above:* Sara guilty, but laughs it off]—which is it?—it isn't me for you wouldn't have the heart to part with me, you need me to look after you" "Listen to him!" "It can't be Wolfe here for you know very well he wouldn't look at the Queen of Sheba herself, much less marry her, for that would involve him in the game, as he calls it, and make him start living. Isn't that right, Gentleman?" W[olfe]. smiles "Exactly. I hereby make over my share in women to you, Honey" "But maybe I'll hold you to that promise some day. And it won't be Jonathan, will it, Mother? He's too busy scheming how he'll grab the world away from whoever owns it to bother—unless the girl's father owned the world and he'd see marrying her as a shortcut. But this girl's father only owns ships so—It must be Ethan then, Mother. He's a sailor & she'd be in his line" Nancy interposes indignantly "Nothing of sort—I've met her—she's spoiled, proud, cold as ice—and delicate—her health's excuse for voyage although I think that's only pose, she thinks makes her interesting—oh no, not the wife for Ethan at all—he needs someone healthy & warm & loving, able to take care of him" (Steward comes in carrying bags) "Ssshh—must be them now" Capt. P[ayne]. comes in with Warren & Elizabeth—introductions— Payne & Nancy accompany them to cabin—Sara remarks "she does look like proud piece—but Ethan is proud too—and she's beautiful"—Honey laughs—Payne comes back [*added above:* Sara "when sail?"—"soon now—two other cabin passengers due—but won't wait—who are they?—man & wife]—congratulates Sara on E[than]'s promotion—but confesses it's Nancy's doing—turns back to cabin as Eliz. & Nancy & Warren come out—Sara (aloud[?]) "He's a decent, pleasant old man—but a blind old fool all the same" "What do you mean, Mother?" "Nothing"—as others rejoin them, steward comes in with bags —then Graber & Leda come over—he is drunk—her appearance strikes everyone into stunned silence—Graber follows steward blindly, "come on, m'dear," goes into cabin—she stands

looking from one to another with a mocking, amused defiance
—then says "good morning"—the Capt., flustered, feels called
upon to make introductions—"Mrs. Graber, isn't it?"—she is
introduced to the women—she gives each a searching glance—
to Sara, smiling "I *am* glad to meet you. I'm sure we'll understand each other" to Nancy "Yes, I think I know you"—to
Elizabeth, who snubs her, sharply "You are not fooling me.
I know you, too—and what you want from me" "I!" Warren
starts to splutter. She says to Capt. "You needn't bother introducing the gentlemen, Capt. I have met them all before" (she
laughs) "needn't look so embarrassed. I mean others so like
you it makes no difference." (then to Ethan) "Except you.
No, I've never met you before—but I will now, of course"
Ethan smiles, pleasantly amused, "I think not" She smiles "You
do. Well, we'll see." Graber sticks his head out of stateroom
"Goldie [*i.e.,* Leda], aren't you coming?" "I'll be right there,
Ben" She bows "I'll have the pleasure of seeing you all later"
(She goes in) Warren sputters, rebukes Capt for introducing
daughter. Eliz. remarks coldly, commandingly "Never mind,
Father. The lady made no impression on me whatsoever" (then
forces a laugh) But I admire her impudence. What I want
from her indeed!" (She gives a little shudder of disgust) But I
do feel the air will be a bit purer out on deck. Such rank beastly
perfume! Are you coming, Father?" She goes out. He says indignantly to Capt. "Graber! Did you hear? An actress—or
maybe even out of a house—before she married. If I had known
she was to be fellow passenger I'd have had the office tell her
we were full. Well, have to make the best of it. I've no doubt
she'll keep to herself." Ethan comes in to report tug standing
by—Much commotion & Hull comes in—insists he's able to
make trip—finally Capt. consents, apologetic to Ethan but secretly relieved—puts it up to owner on side—owner half & half
"I've often thought you could make speedier voyage—but of
course, safety ship, passengers, no repair bills—and Hull's long
service with you, etc."—Hull caustically to Ethan, afraid I'll
have to trouble you move your gear back to your own cabin."
Ethan seems about to explode—Sara "Ethan" He turns to Hull
"Very good, sir—and I congratulate you on recovery"—Capt.
heartily approves, that's a fine lad—and now—he gives orders

146

—Ethan & Hull out and he & Warren follow. (Goldie [*i.e.,* Leda] has come in and witnessed interview. Graber comes out) —Sara laments for Ethan—Nancy furious, Hull did it just in spite, finally bursts into tears—Goldie [*i.e.,* Leda] pats her on back—never mind, I don't like that Hull, I know his kind, they never want to admit they're too old, they'd like to murder youth—but perhaps he'll fall overboard or we can give him a push" Nancy horrified. Honey laughs. Graber greets Wolfe, glad to see someone on board he can have game with—singing starts—company of gold-seekers—ship moving from wharf— Honey says, "come on, Mother—I want [to] join in"—[*added above:* but she stays—he takes Wolfe(?)—] Graber "Come on, Goldie [*i.e.,* Leda]. See last of N. Y.—and maybe I'm not glad to see last of it"—nervous, haunted now—Goldie [*i.e.,* Leda] warns him—sends him out after Honey & Sara—she stays with Nancy—warns her, you shouldn't show your feelings so openly. Of course, the old man would never see, but others have sharper eyes and might tell him." Nancy confused & horrified "Don't know what you mean" "Oh, yes, you do. And you needn't be afraid with me. I'm an absolutely impure woman, you see. It means nothing to me what anyone does or how or why they do it" Nancy stammers—Ethan comes in—Nancy commiserates hysterically—Ethan repelled—Lisa [*i.e.,* Leda] speaks "Introduce me"—Nancy does so—L[eda]. says "Hard luck"—E[than]. stares at her "Yes, it is"—"But luck changes" "When" "Sometimes when you least expect it. And you—I think you've about reached the point where you make it change"— Hull comes down companionway—sneers—entertaining ladies when he ought to be on deck—Ethan tries to be patient, saw a moment when he thought he could get stuff out of cabin— Hull gloats—thought I was finished this time, thought you'd sneak sail on her, and maybe Capt would take sick or, better still, die—Nancy angry—will report him to Capt.—Hull sneers, maybe I'll have report to make to him, too, Missus, I'm older than him but not as blind. (then to E[than]. insultingly) "Get out of here where you belong!" E[than]. turns, meets Lisa's [*i.e.,* Leda's] eyes. She says with contempt "Is this the wonderful discipline on ship I've heard about, that you stand for every insult and are afraid to hit back?"—Ethan whirls—smashes

147

Hull on jaw—Hull falls, hits head on stairs—lies still—Nancy stifles scream—Ethan looks down—Lisa [*i.e.,* Leda] examines Hull—then says simply, dead—Ethan, "Dead?" "Yes, that's what you really meant, isn't it?" Nancy "No—didn't mean kill him, did you, E[than]?"—Lisa [*i.e.,* Leda] sends Ethan out—then to Nancy—"And now you & I will do a little lying. He slipped coming down—we were here—we saw him—hit his head—that's all. You hear me" Nancy staring down at body—with shudder "Yes" "What's the matter? You're glad he's dead, aren't you?" "No, no, how can you?" "Don't be hypocrite" "Yes, yes, I am glad. I am. It's true. Why shouldn't I say it?" "Good! Now you're talking like a real woman. And now you're looking at this dead old man and thinking of another old man and that if only he were—" "No, no, you're horrible. Oh, I hate you. You're evil. Stop putting thoughts in my head. Go away—or I can't help it! I'll scream" (She shrieks and Lisa [*i.e.,* Leda] screams with horror with her—then Lisa [*i.e.,* Leda] grabs her as she is about to faint) "That's good. That's what I wanted you to do—to scream with horror when we found out he was dead. Ssshh! They're coming. Remember what we must tell them now. Nancy bursts into violent sobbing

Curtain

Scene—The same, a few minutes later—The Captain is just straightening up from examining the 1st mate's body—Warren stands beside him—"Well?" "Nothing to do. He's gone"— Nancy breaks hysterically into her lie of how the mate had slipped and fallen—calls on Sara & Lisa [*i.e.,* Leda] to witness —Payne pats her on arm—"I know. You've told us before" (to W[arren].) "I suppose in his condition—heart weak—dizzy spell and fell—" "Yes, a terrible accident" (forces laugh) "Not a very favorable omen to start voyage, eh? I'm glad I'm not superstitious." (Eliz[abeth's]. voice calls down imperiously from door of companionway) "Father! I want to know what has happened! Tell this man to let me come down!" Warren signals to sailor above guarding entrance "No, no!" Sailor's voice "Sorry, Miss. My orders" Warren "I'm coming right up, Eliza- beth—coming right up" to Capt "Suppose you'll send his body back by tug?" "Yes" "I'll keep my daughter out of way. She mustn't see death—never has—terrible shock to one so delicate and highstrung. I'll go to her" (He passes Lisa [*i.e.,* Leda] by companionway. She remarks with drawling mockery "It might do her good. There's nothing like the sight of death—to wake people up and start them living" He stops and stares at her fascinatedly "Yes. One sees there is so little time left—and one has missed so much—and one is growing old" (She gives a little throaty laugh. He snaps out of mood she has cast on him —frigidly) "I beg your pardon, I don't know what you're talk- ing about. Will you kindly let me pass?" "Of course—if you want to"—He goes up companionway—Capt. sends steward for Ethan—Nancy, misunderstanding, breaks out hysterically "why do you want him? What has he to do with it? He wasn't here"—Payne looks at her in surprise—Sara hastily breaks in, "the Captain will be wanting to tell him he's first mate now again and give him his orders" Payne still stares at his wife, in the back of his head an aroused wonder which is the germ of suspicion—He says a bit sharply "Naturally. What else?"

Nancy flustered "Of course. How silly of me! I—" Door at left, rear, from main deck opens and closes, but it is not Ethan but Wolfe—He stands there for a moment—Capt., after glance at him, with head bowed looks down at body with growing grief —Wolfe approaches, looks down at body with cool indifference —Lisa [*i.e.,* Leda] watches him interestedly—He shrugs shoulders, turns away, goes to table, into drawer, mechanically takes out cards and begins his solitaire—Lisa [*i.e.,* Leda] comes and stands behind him—Sob shakes Captain's shoulders. He mutters "Poor Tom—old friend—forty-five years we've sailed the seven seas together—and now—" —Nancy breaks out hysterically "Don't, Enoch! I can't bear it!—He is startled out of his grief—sees Wolfe playing—blazes into anger "Put away those cards, Sir! Damn you, have you no respect for the dead!"— Sara joins in "Yes, Wolfe. Don't be so heartless" Wolfe gathers cards together coolly "Sorry, Captain. You think he cares? It seemed to me the dead are so entirely indifferent to our little games" Lisa [*i.e.,* Leda] laughs, pats Wolfe on the cheek "I like you" Capt. bursts out "It is no question, sir, of what—" Ethan has come in—addresses the Capt. quietly "You wanted me, sir?" Payne turns to him. Nancy bursts out with her story of the fall again—Payne corroborates—Ethan looks down at body calmly—"He's dead?" "Yes" (then angrily) "Damn it, you say that as if you were talking of a dead dog! And you've sailed with him for 8(?) years. Have you no feelings?" Ethan replies calmly "I have no hypocrisy, sir, if that's what you mean. There was never anything but enmity between him and me. I cannot pretend a grief I do not feel." Nancy bursts into sobs "Oh Ethan, how can you be so unfeeling—so cruel to me— (wildly) I mean, to him—to him!" Sara (warningly) "Ssshh! Ssshh!"—Ethan has given her a glance of cold scorn—he turns to Capt—"I am to be first mate now?" Payne(with resentful anger) "Yes, Mister—for this voyage—I make no promises beyond that—it all depends—and I tell you frankly I wouldn't appoint you now if I had any choice—I—(angrily) "Go take your duties, Mister—and I want to warn you—no trickery on your watch—no sneaking sail on her when I'm asleep—for I'll wake—obey my orders strictly, Mister—or, by God, I'll put you for'ard among the crew!" Ethan says unruffledly "Very

good, sir" (turns [*added above:* and starts up companionway])
"Wait—you seem to profit by misfortune—second mate fractured skull—now the 1st mate—I suppose now you're hoping
I'll fall too, & break my head and then you'll have your ambi-
tion, you'll command her, rack[?] her to pieces to break record". Nancy runs, throws her arm around neck hysterically
"No! Don't say such things! Ethan doesn't want you dead—
why, it's like saying I want you dead" (She kisses him, sobbing.
He is immediately ashamed of himself, holds out his hand to
Ethan) "I'm sorry, my boy, I'm sorry, Ethan. I'm upset. Forget it" (Ethan shakes his hand) "Of course, sir. If you don't
want me any further, I'd better—" "Yes, take over, Mister"
(Ethan goes. Payne breaks from Nancy—got to go on deck—
tells Sara take her to cabin—he goes up companion—Sara starts
with Nancy toward cabin—Lisa [*i.e.,* Leda] pats Nancy on the
back, "not so bad for a beginner, but you'll have to do better—
before this voyage is over".—Nancy looks up, stares fascinatedly into her eyes, bursts out in an excited whisper "Yes—I
made him believe, didn't I—he'll never guess, will he—he'll
never guess" (then horrified at herself [*added above:* to Sara])
"Oh—take me away—make her go away!" (hides face on Sara's
bosom)—Sara stares at Lisa [*i.e.,* Leda] "I'm thinking you're
a strange hard woman—but not half as hard as you'd like to
make out" Lisa [*i.e.,* Leda] laughs "You think so? Maybe so.
Maybe not. What's the difference?" Sara crosses herself—afraid
it's unlucky voyage—"What is bad luck for one makes good
luck for another—and it all winds up even in the end" Sara
takes Nancy into cabin. Wolfe has taken out his cards & begun
to play again. Lisa [*i.e.,* Leda] turns to him. He says quietly
"I feel something in the air. What is it? Did Ethan murder
our friend there?" "Don't ask questions. You don't really care
whether he did or not, do you?" "No—except I'm interested in
seeing Ethan get what he thinks he wants in order to watch
him throw it away" "And what do you want?" "Nothing" "Not
even me?" "Not even you" "I'll make you before we're through.
Want to bet?" [*Added above:* I never bet, I only play for nothing" "Afraid you'd lose?" (Stung) "I'm not afraid of anything!
I'll take any bet you like. But] "I have nothing" "You have
yourself" "That is the greatest & commonest illusion." "Eh?"

"But if you accept it, all right I bet myself" "Against myself"
"Done!" "Done" (Honey & Graber enter, singing "Sacramen-
to")—Graber, very drunk, saying gold-seekers for'ard good
fellows but fools—Honey tipsy singing—Graber thinks mate
drunk—indignant officer of ship in such condition—Leda
shocked into indignation—bawls him out, man dead—Graber
immediately terrified—rushes to her, clings to her for protection—she soothes him contemptuously—Honey awed, crosses
himself—Graber whispers L[eda]'s ear—She says "Shut up that
superstitious junk—has nothing to do with you—God, to think
I'd ever get tied up to man with conscience!" Wolfe (quietly)
"Bad singing—but dead only ones it can't disturb, I should
think"—L[eda]. takes this as reproach, becomes flip again—
Rev. Dickey enters—says Capt. told him come here—[*Opposite:* Ship starts from dock just after Dickey's entrance?] L[eda].
breaks in mockingly "Yes—something in your line—show us
your best stuff—take curse off this voyage—will join in the
hymns—you may not believe it but I had the strictest kind of
religious bringing up—I owe all my success to that—" (He
stands gaping at her in shocked horror) "you don't believe me.
Listen!" (She sings "Fields of Eden")—Graber & Honey laugh
& applaud—Dickey turns back on them, kneels by corpse, begins to pray

Curtain

Scene—The Clipper becalmed in the South Atlantic in late November—evening—looking astern from the main deck at the break of the poop—reveals interior of Ethan's cabin at right, center, front and interior of after cabin. In Ethan's cabin, he is discovered lying asleep on bunk, almost fully dressed, turns restlessly in sleep. On poop deck above, grouped to right and left of mast, are, counting from right to left, seated on deck chairs, [*added above:* Nancy] Sara, Jonathan (to right of mast) Warren, Elizabeth & Dickey—opening discussion the calm, its unusualness here at this time of year, great disappointment in its halting record passage to and over Line and tying "F[lying]. C[loud]'s" record to Tropic of C[apricorn].—already feeling of tension, stifling air, stagnant sea, impotent rebellion against a malign fate—and a turning against Captain & toward Ethan—after all record passage to Line was sheer luck, there never was such a favoring wind, he was forced into a record, he even seemed to resent it or be afraid of it—and from Line to Tropic if he'd cracked on they would have crossed Tropic days ahead of "F[lying]. C[loud].", they could afford this calm—and row Capt. had had with Ethan for setting more sail in his watch without orders, Warren had thought Capt. right at time but now—"not one to approve recklessly going after record for record's sake but in these slack shipping times when record is thrust on one it's duty to get that ad[vantage]., to follow one's luck"—Jonathan says impatiently "There is no luck, one makes luck with one's will" (then flatteringly) "I'm sure that's what you've done in your success, sir"—Warren pleased—Nancy speaks up as if coming out of dream "You think one must make one's opportunities for—for happiness. But that makes life so terrible" Jonathan says no, that's all that makes life worth living. Dickey "not very Christian sentiment—bow to will of God—but, of course, if you mean take every opportunity to seek grace, to save own soul"—Jonathan (dryly) "Know nothing of soul—what shall it profit—" "Oh come now. That's blasphemy" Eliz. "I don't think it is, I believe what I want in this life"—Jonathan pleased, Nancy strangely moved—He turns to her "And happiness is beside my point. One sees one's goal, fixes on it, then devotes one's life to reaching it. Happiness or unhappiness are by-products of one's striving"—Nancy "That's for a man—but for a woman"—appeals to Sara—Sara says meaningly "a woman often finds happiness by accepting unhappiness"—Nancy rebellious—no, I used to believe that but now I know it's a lie"—Eliz. "Well, I'm a woman and I quite agree with J[onathan]. Happiness is beside point. And when women talk of happiness I've always discovered they mean only one thing, love" Nancy (flustered) "Oh, no. I wasn't—I meant, everything"—Eliz. "I'm a woman and love isn't important to me"— Jonathan "Take Ethan, now. He's an example of what I mean—he wants only one thing—prove power over sea which to him is life—make record—be at top—admires will but thinks goal nonsense—still, point is what does he care for happiness, his own or anyone else's—or for love"—Nancy objects violently, doesn't know Ethan as she knows, he's not inhuman monster he makes out"—Sara comes to rescue, she's not well, go to cabin and lie down—Nancy goes—after she's gone Sara makes excuses to men for her, this calm, stifling heat, her bad nerves —Eliz. says with contempt "she's a fool, that woman—a silly fool to show as plainly she's a fool" Warren teases "so old & wise & cryptic. What do you mean?" Eliz (to J[onathan].) "You know what I mean" "Yes, I do" "It's all fault that horrible Mrs. Graber. She talks to her. How can she. One should ignore her" The men all embarrassedly defend Leda, not so bad as they thought, keeps to herself, minds own business" Eliz. "That's just what she doesn't do. I can feel her prying—and you can tell at a glance what she must have been, what she still is—" W[arren]. protests "You can't say that—no proof—(then reprovingly) besides what can you know, of such things?" "Nothing, of course, Ethan [*i.e.,* Father?] I only mean she's evil"— You understand (to J[onathan].)—"I understand it is best to ignore her, as you said"—Eliz. (quickly) Yes, of course, in practice I do. I haven't spoken a word to her. I cut her dead" —Leda comes forward on left to end of rail—turns to walk back, pleasantly "Good evening, gentlemen" All mutter "Good evening" Eliz. stares at her with cold ferocity, fascinated—Leda returns stare, then asks mockingly "Yes? What do you want?" She laughs and walks back. Eliz. breaks out furiously "There!" You see! she insults me continuedly with her disgusting—" Warren (impatiently) "You bring it on yourself. You deliberately provoke it. Why do you always stare at her like that? You were saying why doesn't Mrs. Payne ignore her. Why don't you?" (flustered) "I—I can't—there's something—I mean, look at her, you can't help seeing her" Warren "Don't look at her then" (He gets up—changes subject back to heat, calm & singing—hears Honey's voice—Warren disapproves to J[onathan] —J[onathan]. laughs with affection, Honey plays clown but very shrewd fellow, laughs, sings, jokes & people tell him all he wants to know—he's going to mines, getting all information they have"—Dickey "Graber—worse influence than L[eda].— drunk & gambling all time"—Warren "Remember now where I heard his name—bank upstate went bust—suspect same man off to seek new fortune"—then to calm again—foreboding— seem to have escaped curse of 1st mate's death but now— damn it, if we'd only move, etc." Eliz. "That woman's presence on board" "Nonsense. Let's walk back & speak to Captain"— Dickey & Warren go. Eliz. & Jonathan follow [*Opposite:* They go here leaving L[eda]. with Sara—scene between them—Eliz. goes below—scene between her & Nancy—Nancy to stateroom ("I thought you were going to stateroom to lie down")—Eliz. knocks on Ethan's door—he lets her in—scene between them with door open—Nancy comes out, jealous spying—Leda comes down, catches her—sends her away scornfully—wear heart on sleeve no way—Eliz. comes out—scene, for moment, her & Leda—then her & Ethan—"Well, what do you want? Me? But it will cost you money, you know. Or maybe not, I'm on vacation, resigned, happily married—and you're not bad looking I'll come in, if you like" Ethan "Something about you as evil and unscrupulous as sea—as simple"—"partners in crime"— "well, you love sea, don't you"—afraid Nancy would be jealous?—(angry) what do you mean?—I suppose you'll tell me you're not sleeping with her?"—violence—but she is sceptical and unimpressed—and he stops, baffled—then she asks, if not, why not?—a fool can see she wants you—etc.—doing her a wrong—you're full of talk about sea but it teaches you to take what you want—he is impressed—pretend I'm her—kisses him —in rage, he shuts door on her—Nancy comes out—asks indignantly, what did you mean by saying that to me—then scene Nancy & Leda]—Sara says she will stay—Sara alone—thoughts —J[onathan]. & Eliz. seem take to each other—well, it'd be good match for him—evidently Ethan's not interested—this brings her to Nancy—she's making a fool of herself—"I'll have to speak plainly to her"—Below Nancy comes forward frightenedly to Ethan's door—wants to knock—hesitates—Leda appears behind her—she says "I wouldn't do that if I were you. Never run after them. That's no way to play the game. At least, you've got to make them think they're running after you"— Nancy shocked, indignant, "I [*added above:* feel faint—heat— calm—] only wanted to see if Ethan was awake because I want to ask him—" "About the weather? I know"—she waves this aside—asks impatiently, why can't you be frank, then I might be able to help you get what you want. I'm all for women getting what they want from men." "I—I don't know what you mean—I don't want anything" "You want him. You want him to want you" Nancy (giving way) "No, I—he[?] is" "It's no good lying to me." "Yes. I love him" "Love? Well, I suppose that's as good a name for it as any other—you keep following me around—you want to be frank but you keep beating around the bush—what are you afraid of, that I'll think you're a bad woman? No women are bad to me except the fools that let men keep them from what they want"—"I'm afraid of your telling about 1st mate" "What? I tell? I've never squealed on anyone. And what is it to me. My only feeling is he was an ornery old crab and is better off dead. Don't tell me you're suffering from a guilty conscience" "Yes—I see him lying there—in dreams" "Why? He would have died soon anyway—and, even if your Ethan—" "My Ethan!" "did want him out of his way in his heart, he never thought a smash in the face would do it" "Yes, it was hitting his head, wasn't it—an accident" "Forget it. I hate women with guilty consciences. It's too silly. Where do you think I would be if I harbored a conscience?"—then she goes on to say, doesn't usually give a damn other women's affairs but, maybe it's being cooped up in this ship, what happened when I first came aboard, feel all on ship are mixed up, especially you and me—maybe tonight it's calm, heat, that damned song & sea makes me want to talk—feel sorry for you —like my own experience—good family, small town, well off, father owned [*added above:* carpet] mills, died when I was kid —she married friend of father's, mother's dying advice, he had handled business—17, when girls get crush on older men, 30 years older—loved like father—then disillusion—he wanted money & body—that shocked me then—now I know it's all men ever want—usually separated—" Nancy "No"—"I grew to hate him. I got to feel like a young whore who was keeping an old pimp. It made me laugh, it was so idiotic. I used to lie in bed beside him and pray that he'd die every night. I suppose you do that, too?" "No!" "Why not—only natural. I thought you were going [to] be frank" "No—I—yes, I try not to—but I can't help—" "Of course you can't—any more than you can help wanting Ethan in bed with you instead" "No (then furiously) Yes. I do. I do" (she weeps)—Leda goes on "One night I made up my mind if I was going to be a whore I was at least going to have some pleasure out of it, and make men pay for bringing me pleasure. So I left—New York—men have kept me ever since—not old men, young men—I've been able to pick and choose—and it's I who have always left them [*added above:* until I had enough]—I suppose you're wondering about Graber—well, he's an exception [*added above:* a reaction]— I don't give a damn about him but he's such a slob I felt sorry for him." Nancy "You make love into nothing but—bodies" L[eda]. "And what else is it? And why not? Bodies are all right, aren't they—healthy, natural. Aren't we animals? Can you go to bed with a soul? Poetic drivel aside, love may start in heaven but it goes on or it dies in bed. You want to go to bed with Ethan, don't you—more than anything else in the world?" "No—yes, I do. I do!" "That's better. Why be ashamed of it. He's handsome. Well, I'll help you. I know the game. He may be strange, different, but he's a man. He's all wrapped up in himself, he's off in clouds, we've got to get him down to earth, get him to see you not as a family friend but as a woman.

Once he does, you're pretty, you're still young looking—but [*added above:* it's your fault, you've got to stop pretending to yourself and to him] you must stop playing the family friend, stay in background, you keep too near him, he can't see you—and I'll talk to him, I'll bring his thoughts down to earth and flesh—why do you look like that—don't you trust me—I don't want him—I give you my solemn word as between women, I will do nothing that isn't with the object of making him want you—go to your stateroom now—I'll wait and talk to him—you keep door open—then when I'm finished you come out—hurry now—almost eight bells—I hear him moving around in there—Nancy goes—then turns around— "I—it isn't true— I couldn't—you've made me say things, think things—" Leda "All right. Blame me if you like—but go away"—Nancy bursts into tears [*added above:* I hate you. You're filthy.] goes to stateroom. Leda "But I notice she left door open a little". She sits waiting. Above Captain joins Sara—grumbling—"passengers talk as if I could change weather—make wind blow"—disappointed but coldly satisfied—"this will teach your son, Ethan —fate—sea—his foreboding, knew luck couldn't last—calm unusual here—first mate's death—not superstitious but strange [*added above:* every time he goes down stairs, thinks of mate, fear of slipping]—apologizes for quarrel with Ethan—really like the boy but ship comes before everything—then pumping her, comes around to love—perhaps he's in love—Leda or Eliz. —Sara encourages, thinks he's an eye on Leda—Capt. approves—relieved—but really wants to talk to her about Nancy —strange this trip—seems unhappy—has she confided in you? —no—seems to dislike me, as if I'd done something [to] offend her—Sara says, maybe she feels you're too much wrapped up in ship, take her for granted, etc.—Payne wants [to] believe this—confesses his misgivings, getting old, etc. Eight bells— Ethan comes out—face to face with Nancy—she stammers, so frightened, this calm, etc.—he takes her in arms—suddenly they kiss—then both sorry, guilty—he goes—rushes up to deck to Payne & Sara—Payne very good to him—goes—Ethan guilty —Sara pointed remarks about what good man Payne is—to hell with his goodness—Below Nancy follows steps to companionway—if he'd only fall—! —she says, oh, I can't face him now, he'll want me to go to bed with him, the fool, the disgusting old fool, he'll never die, oh I want Ethan—she rushes out to main deck by ladder—(or he comes down by starboard ladder when she rushes out past)—Ethan to mother, desperately "This God damned calm" envies sea—

Curtain

Scene—Tenth day of the calm—The section of the clipper, from
break of poop to end of wheelhouse, as seen from a point to
starboard on main deck level. The spanker and mizzensails are
both set, spanker boom going off, left rear, mizzensail sheeted
tight against starboard rail, extentinding[? *i.e.,* extending] diagonally off toward right, rear. [*Added above:* The interior of the
wheelhouse is revealed.] On main deck, interior of Nancy's
stateroom, cabin view, and Leda's stateroom. Discovered: On
poop deck: In wheelhouse, the helmsman, Capt. Payne, Graber
& Warren playing cards—on deck near wheelhouse, Elizabeth &
Dickey—on deck forward of mizzensail, Sara & Jonathan—in
Nancy's cabin, Nancy—in Leda's cabin, Leda & Honey—in
recess, Wolfe playing solitaire. This scene should have the feeling of running simultaneously, a subject being picked up from
one to another. It starts in Leda's stateroom, where she is just
finishing dressing after giving herself to Honey. The song of
goldseekers, followed by chanty. Leda pats Honey on cheek,
laughs "Happy now, that you've got what you wanted?" [*Added
above:* "But I guess you're always happy anyway] "Happy?"
He bursts into hypocritical blarney about her beauty, etc. She
laughs "And of course that's all talk to make me feel it would
be too low of me to mention money" He says, has no money,
but he'll find slews of gold in Cal[ifornia]. and give her a hatful
of nuggets". She laughs "I like you. You'll get on. You'll promise people the moon and get them to give it to you" Honey
grins "I hope so" "And you'll never have guilty conscience.
That's why [I] gave myself to you. You're refreshing—you get
fun out of it and I get your fun and my own—so it's I who
owe you something. You're the only one on ship who doesn't
want everything to be more than it is and doesn't blame himself
because it isn't" etc. Song comes—her nerves break—curses
song and calm & captain—this outburst comes like wave over
group—in wheelhouse, Warren comes, bawls out Captain, make
them stop, if I were captain—Capt. hurt but replies calmly—

tempers of crew & gold-seekers getting out of hand—singing a safety valve—He turns to helmsman—steerage way?—no—Warren says, no breeze yet?—no—"and you don't even know where we are!"—no sun, stars, couldn't take reading—Warren says "You mean you haven't found a way. There's always way —if you have will enough, concentration, drive to go ahead, if you're not too old and tired." not young yourself, sir—"man as old as he feels, sir" (switch to Eliz. & Dickey)—she bursts out—damn their song!" "Miss Warren!" "good Bible word—damn ship, damn cabin"—then apologizes "nerves, if only sun would shine, everything dead, no present, no future, only the past, dead, too—feel as if there was a fire inside me, as if I'd have to scream with pain" "I know. You must pray" "Pray. That's your business, I've lost faith in God." "You don't mean that."—soothes her, strokes her arm amorously—she stares at him (switch to Jonathan & Sara)—he springs to feet, looks over side, curses, going backwards—these tubs at the mercy of nature—I want to live see the day when they're wiped off sea, I will, too, I'll help it along, etc.—Sara surprised, always thought he had sea water in his veins—he controls himself—she says only way is forget present, make plans for future—"I've noticed you making up to Eliz & I know she likes you. That'd be a good match." "I know it would" "I think she's no feeling left for Ethan and it's certain he's none for her." "I don't care about that. I'm not looking for love—she has money, brains—strictly business proposition." "I think marriages are best that way" "What are you worried about, Mother? Not about Honey making eyes at that trollop, are you? He isn't serious. He'll never be about anything, etc" "You know it's not that" "About Ethan & Nancy?" "Yes" "I am, too—afraid she'll make fool of him. Too bad the old captain can't die. That would solve matters." "Yes" "The old fool! If he'd managed his ship right. He's too old. I'd like to see Ethan get his chance, etc." (switch back to Eliz. & Dickey) She says coldly "I don't think even a minister should stroke a lady's arm that long" He confused, embarrassed "You said prayer was my business. But I have prayed—prayed & prayed to God—What were you praying for? I have noticed you can't keep your eyes off that harlot when she's around"—he denies, every soul a soul to him, no right to judge, thinks they may wrong her, she seems a mild, good natured creature" "Rats! You know better! If you don't, you're fool. She'll end up by committing fornication with every man, perhaps even including—" "Miss Warren. Really, you forget—" "I heard my father leave his stateroom last night & go to one across the cabin." "Oh, no—you must be wrong— I'm sure—" (switch to wheelhouse) Warren "As I said, a man is as old as he feels. I feel young. I am young in spirit, I could prove it to you by relating a little adventure—(with sneer at Graber)—but perhaps it would be in bad taste in the presence of our friend here." Graber doesn't seem to hear. Absent-mindedly "Will you bet, sir?" "Yes, by God, I insist on cutting. Your luck is too uncanny—and you don't know how to play, damn you—you make the stupidest mistakes as if you wanted to lose—and yet you keep moving ahead of me. I'm not used to that, sir. I've always won, I've always beaten people. It's the cursed luck of this calm, this calm—the trouble with you, Captain, is your mind is not on voyage. You're worrying about other things, your personal affairs, not your duty to ship, its owner, its freight, its passengers—" Capt. furious—if Warren were not passenger—then controls himself—I leave it to you to ask yourself if honorable insult."—He turns and goes out— Warren says sorry, I apologize (then to Graber in loud voice) "He's too old, too old to be captain of ship, too old to be husband. He ought to resign, step down, let young Harford try and get us out of this mess." Graber "He'll hear you—but I suppose you want him to" "Yes—something must be done— we can't just sit back and grow old in this calm of death. But let's play. What card did I lead. I'll confess I don't like cards. I don't like losing. I don't like you. I'm only playing to avoid my daughter. She suspects—never mind what, only this night, you see. I don't know what young girls are coming to. In my generation, a girl would have died of shame rather than let such a thought enter her head, especially about their father" (confidentially) Listen, Graber. In this strange situation we're in, we might be frank, eh? Tell me now, you're not really married to Leda, are you? "No" "Ah, I thought not, sir. Otherwise, your calm would be hard to understand" "I asked her to marry me but she wouldn't have me" "Ah well, nothing to say to

162

that. My play, isn't it—let me see" (switch to Dickey & Eliz) Eliz. "I am not mistaken. He went to her stateroom. I tell you she is turning this ship into a brothel. I will wager there's a man in her stateroom right now" He loosens collar "Really stifling tonight. Miss Warren I know my profession hasn't much to offer, (bitter) God doesn't pay very well. I think in Cal[ifornia]. I may go to the mines, in fact if you say the word, I would do anything, for you are very beautiful and disturbing, and I love you." Eliz. (scornfully) "Don't be a fool. I am through with love. I will marry a man of brains and ability who will be rich, whom I can help with my brains to become rich. That is all I care for now. I am afraid that whore has possessed you as she has everyone, almost. I advise you to take your proposal to her. (then violently) "It is all the fault of this fool of a Captain. If he would keep a decent discipline on his ship—but how can you expect a man who is too old and weak even to control his own wife—" "You think she—" "With Ethan—of course" "Yes, I admit her actions are exceedingly suspicious. Yes, he is a weak character, he" (sees captain) "ssshh" (He tries to lead her back. She breaks away) "No. I am going forward to find Mr. Jonathan Harford—a man of brains and ability—and please don't follow me. Go below to Leda" (She goes forward to Jon[athan]. & Sara. He avoids captain and goes astern around rear corner wheelhouse—(switch to Capt. standing over Nancy's room)—his thoughts—declares faith her innocence, but doubts, rage at Ethan, then hopelessly can't doubt his feeling that she loves Ethan [*added above:* (Dickey comes to him—talks with moral indignation as if blaming him—calm is punishment of God for sin on ship)] (then switch Nancy)—can't sleep—longing for Ethan—why doesn't he take her—they've both pretended long enough— then contrition—poor Payne loves her so—but what do I care? I hate him, I hate him, etc.—then horrified at self—no better than a whore like Leda—(switch to Leda & Honey) Honey (jokingly) "hope she got good price from Warren last night— yes, and I put it in his mind to play cards with Ben—B[en]. having run of luck & gives me all his winnings—Honey says never saw such luck—She says "Unlucky at love, eh? Funny thing is he wants to love—guilty conscience—committed big sin, never mind what, for her—is only playing & drinking so as not to think"—then he is inquisitive about Nancy & Ethan—"don't know—hope so for her sake—your brother is inhuman" [*added above:* & for captain's sake—what do you mean—nothing—] "Yes, faithful to sea. He's crazy" She shows her great interest in Wolfe. He laughs, there's one you'd never get, no use hoping" She says "He & I'd be a perfect couple—he gives as little a damn about anything as I do"—they go out just as Ethan comes out of his stateroom at rear of recess—he sees them—he comes forward to Wolfe in recess—Wolfe endlessly practicing shuffling—Honey joins them—Ethan says with bitter contempt to H[oney]. "must be fine to be nothing but a belly and a sexual organ"—Honey grins, unembarrassed "It is, surely. But you don't do me justice. I've a most melodious singing voice, too" "And the gift of plausible gab" "Don't disparage that, for you'll find you need it before long—boys up forward getting hot & unless a breeze comes soon. It's lucky for captain I'm not unscrupulous" "You!" "I could get myself elected Captain this minute. Think that over"—as for lying with Leda, isn't a living woman better to love than the sea or a damned wooden tub—advises him to try Leda, in her arms he can forget his dream of a record—Ethan disgusted—Honey asks Wolfe when he's going to put his card practice to use—ought to join game upstairs—Graber's luck won't last—he can make some money. [*Added above:* I'll back you.] You won't? Afraid, are you?" Wolfe stung—Honey adds another taunt—goes out entrance main deck, singing—(switch Sara, Jonathan, Elizabeth)—Sara calls to Honey, saying not to get drunk—he returns joking answer—she laughs, makes excuses for him—where has he been all this time, I wonder—Eliz. says down with Leda—then protests to Sara she should complain captain, Leda corrupting her son—Sara says she can't corrupt anyone doesn't want to be corrupted—Eliz (primly) I disagree. She's a very evil woman—puts thoughts in your head—I mean, in men's heads— (Switch to Captain & Dickey. Leda standing at rail by sail)—Dickey says—"you should speak to her, Captain. It's your duty." "Why not yours?" "To be truthful, I'm afraid of her. She's beautiful. She wouldn't believe me. I'm too young. But you are an old man, old enough to be her father"—Payne

164

stung "I'm as old as I feel. I'm young. I'm strong. I could break you over my knee with one hand. I'm not afraid to speak to her"—goes to Leda—begins to rebuke her sternly—she smiles, "you talk like old man, Captain—what would your wife think hear you talking such old man's talk—she wouldn't love you any more, etc.—but I know that silly old shy priest put it in your head—because you're not old—you're young in spirit— man old as he feels—I'm sure you feel young—worth 2 young men—he gives way—she says, not old to me—he says, if I were not a married man in love with wife, I would ask you let me come to your stateroom"—"All right, I'll expect you—but it will cost you money" "It doesn't cost the young money" (sharply) "Remember I've warned you. No more monkey business on my ship" (leaves her—moves back to rail near wheel-house)—she laughs—(switch to Sara, Jonathan & Eliz) Eliz— looks back—"there's that harlot now—coming forward—let's go to the stern"—Jonathan "Come on, Mother—exercise"— they come back—Leda meets Eliz[abeth]'[s] stare—"Why hate me? Men would want you, too, if you'd only give them a chance" "Whore" "Don't be so envious!"—Jonathan says "I thought you were going to ignore her"—takes her away—Sara stops "you're right. She has no more blood than a fish. But she's rich —Jonathan marry her—" then guiltily "God forgive me, why am I telling such thoughts to you" "For God's sake, don't you get a guilty conscience, too. You can't fool me. You're a real woman. You want to get what you want" etc.—Sara goes astern —Leda goes forward—Capt. above—his thoughts—old, death wish—sought to slip on stairs [*added above:* he goes in wheel-house]—(switch Nancy's stateroom)—her thoughts—death wish—Leda goes down ladder—(switch Wolfe & Ethan)— Ethan bursts out exasperatedly—what is Wolfe after?—does calm mean anything to him, doesn't he love anything—"no, I keep out of game"—"You & I used to have something under-neath in common—something of father—but now I feel you're lost—and I need to talk to someone"—Wolfe warms a little— says "but what can I say to you. You don't want wisdom. I see in your heart" "What is wisdom?" "You have a great power of love. I envy you. I can't. You could so easily be happy. I have had to put happiness aside & not be interested in it. You

165

could love ship without desiring to own it, you could love sea without desiring to conquer it, you could love yourself without desiring to destroy yourself." etc.—Ethan replies fiercely, "a eunuch's philosophy!—no, possessions, power"—then why don't you possess Nancy?" "Honor" "Yes, exactly"—Ethan grows bitter, coming to point where he believes his dreams all nonsense—"Yes they are—but look out you don't substitute other nonsense for them"—"I might as well rush back into woman's arms—Leda—become an animal like Honey, etc." "That's the other nonsense" "You're a live dead man" "I accept fate" "I'll make fate"—he goes out—Sees Leda—same with Leda & sea—Leda tells him take Nancy—no, guilt there—possession—I want to let go, go down[?], drown, forget—he kisses her—she says no, I don't love you—you want love—you can't evade your conscience & get what you want by sleeping with me & pretending I'm Nancy—etc. (She goes in)—Scene between Wolfe & Leda—short—she taunts him—he is unmoved—only man I really want to sleep with on ship and you scorn me—no, not you, the game—I refuse to play—"I'd like to see what you're made of. I will, too, some day"—she goes [*added above:* Nancy's room—she goes Leda's room—] he [*i.e.,* Wolfe] is disturbed for second—Ethan's thoughts outside—desire use Leda for Nancy, escape in phantoms—comes in—"where's Leda"—gone to room I suppose—look out for other nonsense—Ethan goes Leda's room, finds Nancy—she gets implications why he came there—cries—then effect of room on both—kiss—then guilt honor[?]—we must wait—(eight bells)—he goes out to go on deck by companionway—she goes back to room—Ethan goes to wheelhouse—relieves Captain—Nancy below, death wish—Captain starts down stairs, death fear, death longing—Ethan watching, death wish— Captain goes lower—Nancy calls, denying death wish, "be careful on stairs"—Capt. falls—Nancy shrieks—crowd into pilot house —Ethan says stand back—goes down—drags Captain into Nancy's cabin—"Is he—" "Yes, I think he's dead"—stare at each other—she clasps him passionately in arms—"Oh Ethan, everything all right now!"—Payne groans—Nancy (with utter despair) "Oh, he isn't dead"—Ethan starts to curse—controls himself—bends by body, then straightens up—"No"—they stare at each other over[?] body, same idea coming to each—Nancy says "they know he fell. They'd never know"—Ethan gives in, then recoils—"Good God, are you mad?"—then she denies—"I—I don't know what you mean—what did you think I meant—I only thought I read something in your mind" "I—good God—no—yes—why should I lie to you—for a moment a thought—against my will—but it's too infamous—come—we must get him to bed"—"yes, yes—I'll nurse him—I'll do anything, etc"—Payne groans moves—Ethan speaks to him "You'll be all right, sir—just a bad fall—you slipped, etc."—Nancy kisses him, full of guilty endearments and promises

Curtain

Scene—Looking forward from after end of wheelhouse at level of main deck, showing interior of wheelhouse on poop deck, and interiors of after cabin below, Sara's cabin at left, Captain's cabin at right. It is the 20th day of calm. In the wheelhouse are Warren & Graber playing cards, Wolfe looking on, standing, Ethan by the man at wheel, staring out the open door. At left of wheelhouse, are Elizabeth & Dickey. Below in Sara's stateroom, Sara & Jonathan. In Captain's cabin at right, he lies in bunk with eyes closed, Nancy sits beside his bed her eyes fixed on his face.

In wheelhouse scene repeats pattern of previous scenes except everyone more hectic—Warren losing—catches Graber cheating against himself—flies in rage—no gentleman—humiliating—do you think I'm such a bad loser?—Wolfe says not thinking of you but of himself—Warren bawls Wolfe out, if you want to get in game say so—no—then shut up—wants to lose, indeed! —preposterous—inhuman—crazy—but I think we're all going crazy in this damned calm—taunts Ethan—so they finally got sun today only to find 50 miles behind where they were two weeks ago—a fine record, young man—you with your talk of records—Ethan "I must remind you, sir, I am not in command this ship" Warren backs water, still you might do something"— "Captain still gives orders"—Warren "By God, I'm not superstitious but I think he's Jonah. I wish—But of course I don't mean that. Poor old fellow! He can't help being old, left behind his time. By the way, how is he?" "Better, his wife says. He's resting easily." (Switch to Capt.'s cabin) She is staring in front of her. He opens his eyes and reads her look. She senses it and looks at him and starts guiltily. She says frightenedly "Enoch! Why are you staring at me like that? What do you want of me? You stare as if you were waiting—" he closes eyes—she says "You're better, dear. Ethan says you're much better. I'm so happy, dear" (Switch back to wheelhouse) Warren says, "so he's better, is he?—a miraculous recovery—and he owes it all to that sweet woman—the way she's nursed him —a lesson to all—never sleeps—you haven't slept much yourself in the past ten days, I'll wager, Captain" "I am not Captain. No, I haven't slept much. It isn't a situation where one craves for sleep much."—he suddenly turns on Wolfe fiercely—"for God's sake, stop your infernal pacing—I never saw you so restless before—why don't you sit down, join in the game, do something!" He turns and strides out—comes to rail over Capt[ain's]. stateroom. (Switch to Eliz. & Dickey. She is looking in cabin window) "There is something strange about that Wolfe. I admire him—and I despise him—admire him because he's the only man on board that whore, Leda, can't influence— and I despise him because I feel in him an indifference to women so insulting—By the way, where is that Leda? Up with the crew and the gold-seekers, I suppose. She'll have had every man on ship before—And in there her husband or keeper sits playing—My God, it's all so mad, this calm!" "I've prayed and prayed to God for wind, Miss Warren. But perhaps he sees that my heart is no longer pure." "You mean you too have been with Leda? I guessed it, seeing you no longer paw my arm." "Yes, I confess last night [*added above:* I talked with her and] everything suddenly became innocent and clear to me. It did not matter what I did. There was no sin, no God. Life was innocent and beautiful, without guilt." "I wish she could make me feel that! Oh, it's so hot! I'm stifling! That damned song! I wish she would come back. I hate her. I'd like to kill her, but at least when she's around I feel alive." "But today I know there must be a God and this calm, it is all his vengeance[?] on me for my evil heart." "You fool, you are not that important. You are only half a man. Was I flattered when you pawed my arm? No, only annoyed me. That's proof, isn't it? I'm sure Leda would tell you it was." "Then you think it wasn't important? Oh, thank you, I am so glad, so glad!" He cries "Fool! Nothing you can do, could be important! I am beginning to believe with Leda that nothing matters except to want and to be wanted. If I could only want!" (She looks in window) "Look at my father for moral lesson. I have watched him. He has been cheating for days now. It is the infallible system on which he has built his success. But now it loses, although the

169

other cheats himself & tries to lose. Oh Father, how God must laugh at you behind your back!—she laughs—Warren bangs fist on table—"Your game again. This passes all bounds, sir! —then in another tone—"have you any children?"—G[raber]. doesn't answer—You should thank God, sir. I have a daughter. It is a worse form of slavery than being a husband, this being a father—but, by God, I'm sick of it! I'll marry her off—if I can only get a man to want her—men are attracted to her at first because she's beautiful like her mother, but they soon guess that, like her mother, she's as cold as a dead fish!" She turns away from window with a sobbing cry—to Dickey, pitifully—"it's a lie, isn't it—tell me it's a lie—Jonathan, he loves me, he wants me, doesn't he?—you must have noticed the way he looks at me—and it isn't for my money, is it?"—but Dickey is looking in at game—"I am beginning to think that, after all, gambling is no sin—like to play but have no money— the ministry is the most ill-paid calling—of course, if you were sure of a reward hereafter for doing without in this world— sure of the justice of God—but in this calm one doubts—perhaps God cares nothing about justice for man—I thought it would be a very good thing for me if I could marry you, Elizabeth—with your money & position—the food I could eat, for example—I am very greedy—but I didn't want you—too cold—and so I couldn't make you want—" Eliz in rage "So even you—You dare to tell me that, you pitiful creature, you!" —she slaps his face and turns to go forward just as Leda comes back—stands staring at her—Leda laughs—"Good. I didn't think you had it in you. Perhaps, having gone that far you'll be frank at last and tell me what you want from me" "Want from you? Is it likely I would want anything from a whore like you?" "Yes—professional advice—secrets of the trade—you have wished to sell yourself, but before you can sell you must make men want"—"Many of them have wanted—" "Your hand in marriage for your money? But that's not what you want them to want. You don't want to buy them. You want to make them buy you." Eliz. grows confidential— yes, to be candid, I have fallen a little in love with Jonathan, but he is so cold, I think he may be only after my money"— "Well, give yourself to him" "Give myself!" "Find out if he

170

wants you—if you want him" "But that's disgusting! Still I see
what you mean, if I let him seduce me—he seems like a man
of honor—I would have him then" Leda laughs scornfully "You
need no advice from me. I need advice from you, for I'm still
so impractical as to give myself for nothing now and then. But
you don't fool me. You are only hiding from yourself your fear
that men do not want you because they feel you cannot give
yourself" "I can! I will!" "Then prove it" Leda laughs, starts
to go into wheelhouse—Dickey grabs her arm, whispers "You
are so right, Miss Leda. What shall it profit a man if he give
you up for a supposition like his soul? I shall visit you again
tonight, if I may." Leda laughs, goes into wheelhouse. Warren
says "You have cleaned me out of all available cash, Graber.
I shall have to stop"—Graber says, give it all back to him, play
again, he may win—Leda laughs "Still winning with a guilty
conscience, Ben"—"Yes, I have no luck, Leda" Warren outraged, what kind of man is he to make such an offer, does
money mean nothing, sacred responsibility, criminal scoundrel,
sir, ought to be in lunatic asylum"—then shrewdly "but it is duty
of sound business man to remove money from irresponsible
quarters. I accept your offer—but, of course, as a debt of honor
between us". Eliz. laughs mockingly from outside. Leda taunts
Wolfe "Still afraid to get in the game? But I see you've at least
come up to watch it. That's something" "It means nothing"
"No?" She laughs—goes out rear—[*Added above:* He sits
down at table] Eliz. says to Dickey "That lying whore—I'll
prove to her I can give as well as she" "Yes, better to give than
receive. Jonathan is below, I think—perhaps in his stateroom
alone."—She goes—Dickey comes in wheelhouse—says to
Wolfe "I was like you once. I thought gambling was a sin but
now—" W[olfe]. stares at him for a second coldly. He shrinks
away, mutters "I beg your pardon. My mistake"—Leda comes
up to Ethan at rail over Captain's stateroom—he does not
notice her at first—his thought—"what fools we were when we
had that chance—no one would have suspected"—then guiltily
—"Good God! What am I thinking! Murder!"—Nancy below,
staring at Payne, echoes this, then repentantly asks Payne to
tell her he feels better, I love you, such a good husband. I
would do anything for you, etc."—Leda speaks to Ethan "Why

171

have a guilty conscience? You love ship, you love Nancy, of course you wish he'd die, you'd like to kill him. It's only natural." He says automatically "Yes. I know it's silly to feel guilty. I know we were damned fools"—then with a shudder, staring at her "But one doesn't admit such thoughts" "Why doesn't one? I admit everything—and everyone" "You're a horrible woman" "You said I was like sea" "Sea is horrible to me now. What is it waiting for so contemptuously and surely. What are you waiting for?" "I? For your brother Wolfe to desire me." "You'll wait a long time!" "I've fallen in love with him. Don't you think he will ever cease being indifferent? His indifference makes me despise myself, I feel dirty, and so to lull my guilty conscience, I drown myself in mere lust. But it's no good. No! I don't love him! I hate him for making me despise myself. I have built life on desire for my body, but it is nothing to him, he doesn't want me, and so I'm becoming his slave. But I'll win in the end" [*Opposite:* He says "Love? You speak of love? You mean lust, don't you?" "I never noticed much difference" "You don't know what love means" "You don't— for example if W[olfe]. loved me & he were married to an old fool he didn't love, d'you suppose I'd hesitate a moment to murder for love? Lust is what you've the guts to do to get it"] He says, going down to see [*added above:* how] Capt. is. "I hear he's better" "Yes" "And you haven't possessed Nancy yet?" "I only want what can be mine" She laughs "Poor Nancy! Well, I hope the murder will be soon. I hate this calm"—she goes— left alone, he thinks "I stopped Nancy. She was going to—it was I—she had more courage than I—" (switch to Nancy & Capt)—He speaks "don't want to get well—I want to die—and you know why—I'm dead already—you've murdered me"— "No, don't say that—etc."—(switch to Jonathan & Sara—he is talking) "Yes, it might be a very good match for me—I can use him in my plans—but I think he thinks we have some money and when he finds out I've nothing in that line to offer he'll refuse his consent—and as she's under his thumb" "You think so. I don't. If she loved you—" "Let's not talk of love. She wants to get married to get away from father but she cares nothing for love, cold as ice" "Well then, I'm sure at least she wants to believe you love her. I think you've been too respectful with her." "I see. There's something in what you say but not what you mean. Supposing, for example, I could seduce her—" "I won't have that talk etc." "I'm not talking to you as mother but as head of firm, etc." She says you've no heart in you etc. He smiles "Do you want me to make a good match or don't you? etc. (switch to after cabin) Leda coming [?], Eliz. coming out of Jonathan's room. She says "He isn't there. I waited but he didn't come—or I would have proved to you—" "Good for you. You're coming alive at last"—puts arm around her—let's go in see how Capt is—and let Nancy get out of there for while—take rest—killing herself nursing that old fool" "It must be terrible being married to old man when you love someone else." "Yes, I'd murder him" "Yes, so would I" Leda laughs "You *are* being born" "Yes, I think you are the only one on board who knows what life is about. You—you will teach me, won't you—now that I've been frank with you" "You don't need me now. You can teach yourself" (They knock. Nancy startled) Come in—they go in—ask Nancy come out— she says no—Capt. says go, it's no use waiting. I'm not going to die tonight"—the three women go out—meet Honey who is coming drunk from forward, with bottle—he greets them up-roariously—kisses Leda—Sara & Jonathan come out—Eliz. says "you must kiss me, too—but no, I'd rather kiss Jonathan" —she does so—Honey says "oho, so that's how land lies, I've misjudged you—thought you were dried up stick"—she says "I'm not. Am I, Jonathan? I went looking for you in your room just now. I waited—but you didn't come." "I'll be there later" "I'll remember"—then Honey tells he's committee of one from gold-seekers & crew to demand Capt. resign all power to Ethan —I've convinced the fools he's a Jonah, that as soon as he's out ship will move—and if it doesn't I'll tell them it is and they['ll] believe it—I ought to be politician—come on, let's drink, ladies[?] & then Jonathan & I will deliver the message." Nancy "you can't—shock would kill him" Honey says "And wouldn't that be a blessing?" She says "You're horrible" (bursts into tears then says fiercely "Yes! It would!" They drink. Honey & J[onathan]. go in—but Capt. flies into rage—what, give up ship—never—above Ethan suddenly makes up mind kill Capt —goes out wheelhouse—comes down stairs—they explain to him—to their surprise he takes loyalty to discipline stand—will shoot down anyone who comes[?] back—they go up to wheelhouse to get others come down to party—Honey philosophical, will tell them it's done—they'll believe him—in wheelhouse hands bottle around—in Capt[ain]'s stateroom Ethan gets Capt. to bed—Payne thanks him for loyalty—afraid I've misjudged you—I see I can count on your loyalty in all things—you haven't slept with Nancy, have you?—no—I can sleep—yes—(switch to after cabin)—the women's party—let's be frank—no men around with their codes & pretences we have to pretend to believe in—they all confess themselves of their ruthless lust for giving themselves to power—their scorn of spirit, their essential animalism—this alternates with party in wheelhouse—then switch to Capt.—Ethan whispers "Are you asleep, sir?" "Slipping off—I'm so peaceful now I know—I'm old—you can wait for Nancy—ship—then as he's going to sleep "why do you look at me like that. Never mind. I'm tired. I want to sleep & forget"—in meantime Nancy gets up from women's party—ruthless & cruel—I'm sick of this calm—this death in life—this waiting—I want what I can take from life—now!" (She goes in—sees Ethan advancing with pillow—says fiercely "No! Give me what is mine!" snatches it from his hands—leaps at Payne & shoves pillow over his face—Outside the three women are saying "Men talk a lot about love[?] the fools, and make poetry to laud[?] it because the're all afraid to face it, etc.—Up in the wheelhouse, Honey is singing—then suddenly all join in gold song, even women downstairs—3rd mate comes in—a squall coming—maybe it means wind—he shouts down to Ethan—

Curtain

Scene—Late January—late afternoon (sunset?)—approaching
Golden Gate—gentle [*added above:* warm] wind from starboard
—Scene shows after section of ship seen from starboard as in
Scene Two of preceding act, but no interiors are revealed. Mizzensail diagonal from left, rear to off, right front. All passengers
are on deck with exception of Graber & Wolfe—all in hectic
tense state of excitement and jubilation. Dickey, Warren, Jonathan, Honey? sitting by first deckhouse forward from the wheelhouse—Sara, Nancy, Eliz. & Leda sitting grouped by mast at
break of poop. But these groups are not fixed. Everyone is restless, keep rising, sitting down, the groups intermingle, etc.—
As the curtain rises all are talking excitedly about being almost
in sight of land, they are sure ship will beat the Flying Cloud's
record, the wind has died down it is true but it is from astern
and they are hours ahead of record—remarks are heard from
each group, rising above the general chatter, they are all in-
toxicated by memories of the voyage, the danger, the feeling
any moment they were so close to death, the wild storms, life
at its highest, hero worship for Ethan, he has driven her as a
ship was never driven before, he is a superman, he has beaten
the sea—how lucky the old captain died when he did—forgotten
—hard to remember he was ever on ship—the minister had
married Ethan & Nancy right after he had said burial service
over Captain—like a double ceremony—they had seen nothing
strange in this, it had been Nancy's wish, they understand she
didn't want to wait, she had never loved Capt, she was glad
he was dead, she loved Ethan, it was all so natural—and behind
all their talk is the sense that they are sure Captain was murdered, approve, admire. As a background is the triumphant
song of the gold-seekers, dominating a subdued, beaten sea-
chanty, and the clanking of the pump for the ship has been
driven so hard she is leaking badly.

The sentences & exclamations from the two groups at first
—then a topic is taken up by one group, then by the other—

Warren chuckles over pump, Ethan has racked his ship to bits, she won't be worth a damn, but he can have her tinkered up to run okay and on strength of record, depression or no depression, sell her to England for good price—Dickey laughs—Jonathan, Honey approve—everyone totally immoral—Jonathan later passes this story on to women—Sara approves, "if your father had only had some business resource[?]" etc.—Eliz. proud of father, just like him, he has no honor, he'd cheat the devil —Nancy keeps going back to wheelhouse to kiss Ethan, talk about it, is in a trance of passionate love, says "you don't know what it means to be tied down to old man"—Warren says "of course, he was ten years older than me—I'm young"—Nancy says "It was such a relief when he died."—When she leaves them, Warren "when he died. I guess we all have a strong suspicion the old fool's departure was speeded, eh? But never mind, we'll let the happy lovers keep their little secret."—Jonathan while[?] admiring Ethan's victory, want and get what you want, the end justifies the means" Dickey "Of course. It is written God works in mysterious ways. It would be difficult to justify His means, eh?"—Jonathan says still & all, Ethan's end a dead thing, sail is dead, good as a last romantic gesture. Ethan would make a great success if he only didn't have touch of poet in him"—Warren demurs "Don't be so sure, young man. I begin to believe sail may still have future, after this record" etc.

In the woman's group, there is great praise of Ethan—Sara says it was a duel between him and the sea and he's beat it— my father great duelist, etc.—and it's the touch of the poet in him that makes him dream great dreams of himself as a hero of old and follow his dreams to the end—gets that from father. Nancy says yes, he is a poet, a great poet of love"—Eliz. says yes, one's love must be a poet or he doesn't know how to love. Jonathan is a poet, too, in his way—Sara says, hopes now Ethan has beaten the sea, he'll give it up, dream of wealth and power on land and get that, too, it's more satisfying, for you can't hold the sea, it runs through even a poet's fingers" Eliz "That's Jonathan's dream. Ethan & he will work together." (kisses Nancy) "you & I will be like sisters & Sara will be our mother and we will help our men take possession of the world—and we will possess the world by possessing them" Sara—"Have

you & Jonathan spoken to your father? J[onathan]. so poor.
He may object" She laughs "He can't object now. You have
guessed that, surely. Father wouldn't want a scandal. And that
reminds me, we're forgetting all about Leda. She must be one
of us and she will be, her eye is on Wolfe, and what Leda wants
she takes" Sara "I hope so—wake him up"—"We all ought
to be so grateful to her. I feel we owe her so much. I know I
do. I love her. I bless the day I met her. She taught me how
to awake soul & body. I was so warped in myself, so dead, so
sick. She makes everything so simple & innocent, you see just
what you want, you take it" Nancy "Yes. She speaks and you
forget guilt" Sara "Yes, she's a good woman at heart. She
wants everyone to be happy, to have what they want."—Where
is she?—in wheelhouse watching Graber & Wolfe play—Wolfe
winning all Graber's money & Graber is so pleased but Wolfe
indifferent, isn't human—Eliz. says "Oh, Leda will make him
human. She did me and I was as cold as he is, almost.

[*Added at end of scene but marked for insertion here:* Inci-
dent—Jonathan gets Eliz.—good time speak to father, tipsy,
in genial mood—he & Eliz. come to Warren & Dickey—begins
—so they have come, eh. don't go, Dickey, mean a job for you
soon—he says suppose I ought to [tell] J[onathan]., wait, prove
yourself, get some money, etc. my daughter still young, prop
my declining years—Eliz laughs but I'm not prop, you want
get free of me, and anyway too late to wait"—"Oh, so? Well,
I confess I guessed as much. Suppose I ought curse you, etc.—
but nonsense—I understand hot blood of youth, etc." Dickey
"End is propagation so the means is always justified" etc.]

Ethan comes out—cheers from all—questions—he looks up
at sails—for a second, frowns—then reassured, won't beat record as much as he thought but wind, if faint, is favorable, she's
slipping through water, too bad she leaks, but he can assure
them they'll beat Flying Cloud record by several hours, pilot to
pilot, at least—(says this from break of poop)—mad cheers
from gold-seekers—Warren talks about presenting watch—
Ethan says giving up sea—he's beaten her—etc.—talking to
sea as much as to them—then the streak of calm—all wind
gradually peters out—a moment of dead silence—chanty—
then a wail "wind is dead"—Ethan curses—(Nancy flies into

177

his arms, terrified)—"Ethan! The wind is dying" Ethan "No—
after what we did, she can't do that to us" (He commands)
"Send the wind, I say!" (Wind comes) "You see (to all of
them) it was only a streak of calm—not unusual—make blow
stronger from now in—I'd put more sail on her but every sail
is set now—but don't worry—we will get to Golden Gate faster
than any man has travelled by sea before!" He goes back in
wheelhouse—Nancy comes forward—now reassured, speaks
jokingly of fright, for a moment Dickey doubted God, etc.—
they speak of Nancy as she passes—"it's funny, I was looking
at them together and I felt a chill of horror run down my
spine"—Nancy touches Sara as she passes—Sara shrinks—
"What's matter. Is my touch—" "No, no, startled" "For a moment in Ethan's arms then I felt so guilty—absurd" "Of course,
dear! Why in the world would you feel guilty? You were lovers
& love is worth all it costs!" "Of course!"

Curtain

Scene—The same—some hours later—sunset. A dead calm, clanking of the pump louder & quicker now, chanty powerful groundswell, the gold-seekers' song beaten and exhausted with bursts of desperate assertion. The same groups as before are disclosed on deck. They [*i.e.,* their?] mood is even more strained than in the previous scene, they are still desperately hoping against hope, they alternately curse and implore the sea, they tell themselves Ethan will yet drive them through to a record and then they wonder if this calm isn't the punishment for his crime & Nancy's & Leda's lust—then they fool themselves into thinking the ship is moving, has been moving, that their watches must be wrong, they've only been in calm a short time. Warren tells the minister "Pray, you fool, you! What are you for, anyway? What do we support you for? Pray for success for us and see that we get it or else we'll find a way to get on without you!" Minister says "No use praying—God's punishment for the crime and lust on this ship—gambling"—"How about your own lust—the worst of all—we're only human but you're not supposed to be"—Minister admits this—becomes hectic, revivalist—"we must all repent before it's too late"—calls on them—"I am the greatest sinner in the world but the blood of the Lamb will still wash me clean," etc—they all tell their sins —then singing of hymn—all bow their heads except Jonathan who maintains a sort of grim "I-told-you-so" attitude—it all comes to dead, old-fashioned sail at mercy of sea—with steamers, machines, men won't be depend[ent?] on Nature (sea[?]), they will conquer it—he also calls Sara back to herself when she feels guilt, remembers religion, starts to bless[?] herself— look out for touch of poet in you—she indignantly denies—he tells her keep her head clear, need it on land tomorrow, forget record, it doesn't matter, steamers will smash any sail record to bits within a few years anyway—sorry for Ethan but his own fool fault for chasing rainbows—

Change of attitudes when they all begin to blame sin on ship

—Warren calls Eliz dirty little slut—she says fine example you set, you old whoremonger—he curses day she was born to disgrace him—she curses day she was born of such a father—minister bawls her out and she, him—she shrinks from Jonathan—you beast!—"I? As I remember it was you—" (then calmly) "Keep your head. This will all be good for you, teach you to be a helping brain instead of a sexual organ—kind of wife I want who will be asset, a partner—the animal I can always buy—from Leda's kind"—"It's a lie. It's you who were animal. I was a pure girl. I never dreamed—I never let myself dream—" Nancy in daze of love "Poor Ethan!"—Eliz. (viciously) "How about poor old man who was your husband? Murderer!"—She turns to Sara—Sara condemns her fiercely, for leading Ethan to crime—then says "no! I'll be just. You would have told me to be just, Simon"—then she says to Nancy —"no, what Ethan did, he did of his own will" "But he didn't, he didn't, he is innocent, I alone am to blame" etc.—Nancy goes to wheelhouse—as she passes, each calls after her "murderer"—even Jonathan against her—handicap for him to start under cloud Ethan's disgrace.

At height of his revivalism, minister declares still chance for record if they cleanse ship of sin by sacrificing sinners to the sea (God)—"throw them overboard"—rush from forward—Ethan comes out of cabin with Nancy—red sunset light—howl of execration—then Warren says wait, he wants to announce something—maybe we have beaten record after all!"—Ethan draws pistol—Honey has come out of wheelhouse—"put that popgun away, a waste of powder to shoot fools"—he rushes to break of poop—"Wait, boys. As you see, I'm drunk again"—laughter—minister starts condemn drunkenness—Honey mocks him, crowd jeers—Honey then makes speech in which he says why get excited about record, about sin, ain't we all sinners and proud of it—all ashore tomorrow anyway—gold waiting for you—to hell with this old tub—you couldn't go gold-seeking tonight in dark, anyway—but see there's land, the Golden Gate, and behind it hills full of gold—I promise you you'll all be rich —and you know me, Honey Harford, my word is as good as my bond, etc.—and now you've still plenty of whiskey—why not celebrate the end of this damned voyage?—and you can ask me to have drink with you and maybe I will—and I promise you I'll see that you get everything your heart desires tomorrow"—he goes down to them—they go off forward.

All aft suddenly agree with Honey, become reasonable—Dickey says "Of course, it's silly to quarrel with will of God. He is simply showing us the futility of our little vanities. Making a record wouldn't have saved any souls, would it? A very successful meeting, though—I was in good voice, I had them in the hollow of my hand, should have passed plate—but after all better to leave vengeance to the Lord—and the sinner's conscience—relieves one of responsibility"—Warren talks of selling ship, wracked to pieces, wish she would sink, insurance —to J[onathan].—"you're quite right—sail is dead—steam is future—let's drink—forget voyage—afraid none of us were ourselves—that fool Ethan!—records are good for business but a record for a dead issue[?]—and yet he gets us all worked up over it!"—as for crime we think they committed, no proof, and it's the police's business, not ours—we don't want to be involved as witnesses—I'll fire him though—I wouldn't sleep with a good conscience if I didn't—and he's unfitted for job in the new age, anyway." He calls to Ethan coldly "I hereby fire you, Captain. Your negligence, disregard for my property, safety of passengers, your failure to win the record when it was within your grasp" etc.—Ethan says "Very good, sir. There's a breeze springing up now, if you'll notice. We should sight land soon and be at the Golden Gate by midnight, although we'll have to wait for pilot in morning" He goes into wheelhouse—Nancy cries "Ethan"—follows him in—Minister says "Then we weren't in sight of land—I could have sworn I saw—" Warren laughs "That Honey! He'll wind up in Senate, if he doesn't look out!"

Curtain

Sara not in scene—has gone to stateroom—couldn't bear face it(?)— Eliz. out of scene after talk to Nancy—goes below to avoid her(?)
Or scene ends with Honey's speech (?)
Or Ethan goes back in wheelhouse after his announcement(?)

Scene—From astern looking forward as in Scene Three of
Act Three—midnight—fog—moonlight—a gentle breeze from
astern. Shows interiors of wheelhouse, Sara's stateroom, Captain's stateroom, after cabin. In wheelhouse, Graber & Wolfe
playing, Leda sitting beside Graber as if it were she who is
playing against Wolfe, Honey and Jonathan looking on, Ethan
standing in starboard doorway staring out into fog, Sara in
stateroom (dark?)—Elizabeth by rail to left of wheelhouse.

Wheelhouse—Graber loses—Leda "let's make this short"—
she triples stakes—Jonathan says don't do it, Wolfe. You're
way ahead. It's all to his advantage."—Wolfe stares at him
coldly "your values nothing to me"—accepts bet—Jonathan
"You fool!"—turns away, talks to Honey—crazy fools, both of
them, one happy if he loses, the other indifferent to winning.
It's mad—play the game to win"—Honey says "sshh, Ethan
will hear you"—then his own philosophy "gambling silly unless
you run house—let the suckers give you their money" etc.

Left of wheelhouse—Eliz. thoughts—tries to be cold about
Jonathan—can never forget the joy of her shame—as father
called her dirty little trollop—but did he ever love her—even
want her instead of just a woman—got to know—calls Jonathan—Honey "your lady love calling"—he goes out—affectionate, catch cold, go to bed—she is encouraged but says don't
pretend, you don't love me—Jonathan "don't let's get sentimental"—"You didn't even want me" "man always wants a
woman"—"a woman—but not me particularly, did you—you
only did it so I'd have to marry you—and because you thought
it was what I wanted"—"yes, that's true"—"for my money"—
"No, I'll make own money but to get an opening wedge, yes—
but not all—studied you—except for craziness on voyage, you
are intelligent etc.—you'll make good wife—and I'll make good
husband—won't run after other women" "because you don't
care" "I'll give you power & money. I'll be in your debt at first
but pay back hundredfold—it will be partnership" etc.—she

coldly agrees everything—he says "I think we ought get married tonight—if on trip no one will ever question when" "Yes. I feel dirty little slut who has sold herself for counterfeit" "marriage will cure that"—father comes up—speak to my daughter for moment—J[onathan]. moves off—Warren says, hard for father speak daughter but are you sure?—yes, and we've just been talking, decided get married at once—yes, perhaps best. Dickey awake, I heard him praying in stateroom. Well, I'll be sorry to lose you, Eliz." "Rot! Don't introduce sentiment. You'll be glad get rid and I'll be glad get away from you—I gave myself deliberately—wanted husband—he's got brains, ability, he'll make good, you'll give him a good opening, he doesn't want any money, etc." "Better than I thought. And if he doesn't make good, you can always divorce him." "Exactly." "Well, might be worse. I'll go and arrange matters with Dickey & then call up for you"—He goes—she laughs bitterly "what am I hurt about—after all, I always swore I'd be loved for my brain and not my body. I've got what I wanted" etc. Jonathan has come back in wheelhouse.

Wheelhouse—Graber loses again—Leda again doubles stakes —eight bells—Jackson comes up relieve watch—Ethan oblivious—J[onathan]. pleads with him to go to bed—he gives orders—goes out on deck—speaks to sea—?—Honey speaks to J[onathan].—"he's queer—we'd better watch him"—they go out—Jonathan tries console him practically "you're good loser —and, in long run, this will be good thing—get you off sea— dead issue"—Ethan "you mean well, J[onathan]—but your values are not mine—the sea is a symbol of life to me, etc."— then sharply, I murdered the 1st mate, I murdered the Capt, in order that I might possess life" Honey "Glory be to God, don't say that" "It's true" J[onathan] "You're a fool. You shouldn't trust even us with such a secret!" "You'll be a great success in world, J[onathan].—but a horrible failure in life— but you may not ever realize it" "I'll take care of my life. It's your life—" "I'll take care of that" "I think you're playing the romantic Harford—covering up Nancy" "I killed them" "Well, no one suspects—no one can prove—" "I know" "Not going to confess, are you—got to consider family, our name—hard enough start out here on shoestring without—" "I said you'd be great success. No. I'm not going to confess" "Good. I don't believe you anyway. It isn't possible" "And now that's off your conscience" "Go to bed—get some sleep." Warren calls Eliz. She calls J[onathan]. They go off, rear. Honey breaks down "Good God, Ethan, how could you—But I'm not blaming you. I'll stick by you, to hell with them all, we Harfords'll beat the devil if we stick together" He pats Honey on back "Thanks, Honey. I'm afraid I've felt a superior contempt for you. Forgive it" "Nothing. Sure, I'm nothing much" "Go down to mother, I know she knows, that she's grieving alone. I can't go to her yet—not until I can bring her a decision she'll approve" "I'll go—but hadn't you better go to Nancy. She's alone too" "I have to bring her a decision, too." (then suddenly) "I'm glad this has all happened. I'm glad I staked everything, committed crimes to win, I'm glad I lost. If it were only myself I would know what to do and do it this instant. I'd let the sea possess what it has won and beyond desire for possession, I might find peace at last." Honey "You mean you—don't" (grabs arm) "I said I hadn't come to a decision—what to do with love. Go to mother" Honey goes. In cabin below, Nancy comes from her stateroom into Ethan's—"watch changed, why doesn't he come"—suddenly she sees husband on bed—goes over fall & murder scene—horror, prayer, can't pray—then defiance—don't care, if he loves me—then runs from room— above Ethan says "I've got go down and face her—but I don't love her—only lust to possess—if I could only go down and say I love you—that horror of stricken loneliness in her eyes —to kill a body, what is that?—but I can't murder a soul— and how can one lie to a soul—I can't go to her—temptation jump over—he conquers it—to sea, no, you can't have such a complete victory as that. I will never surrender unconditionally—he goes in wheelhouse to avoid temptation—Wolfe "I thought you wouldn't go without saying good'bye"—"I won't, Wolfe" Leda unnerved "For Christ's sake, aren't you human at all" He smiles at her "Hardly at all, I hope. Humane, rather. My line[?]?" (Switch to Sara's room) Sara sad, desperate & uneasy, glad Honey came—where's Ethan—he says on deck, he's all right—changes subject to talk of Wolfe, winning, devil's own luck, born gambler, get him start gambling house, he doesn't care, he'll do anything you ask—she runs[?] for minute to practical. Yes, my father was great gambler but always lost, only right for Wolfe to win it back—then she's angry at herself and him for thinking—goes back to Ethan—"he says he'll be coming down to you soon—but he's got to decide something first." "Glory be to God" (terrified)—"What's the matter, only about whether he'll leave sea or not" "No—your father would always come to me when—and he'd leave it to my honor— God damn the Harfords—their honor—it's like a devil they cast from themselves to you to possess you with"—then after pause "Oh, Honey, I'm terrified the Captain didn't die—" He tries to deny this, comfort her—she tries to be comforted— (switch to Capt's cabin) Nancy enters again—can't stand it— got see him—calls up stairs—he starts but pretends not to hear—Leda says "Nancy's calling you. She's alone. She's afraid. I can tell by her voice. Aren't you going down? (as he hesitates) For Christ's sake, aren't you human either?" "I'm going" "No, maybe you'd better stay—no, what good would that do? —Triple stakes this time, Ben. "We'll beat him yet" Ethan goes down. Nancy wants take him in her room—where they've loved —forget—he insists on staying there—face it—I'll face anything with you—if you only love me—he lies—kisses her— only desire—he remains himself—he still possesses himself— finally she says—and it—they go all over fall, killing—she takes all the blame—finally she tells what she's decided—take all blame—confess—set him free—he probes her cruelly—for other woman—children by other woman, happiness— absolutely give him up in her head & heart and then still go on—I don't love you—I'd still go on even then because I love you—this breaks him—also pride—think I could accept that—no, will go together, etc.—she believes he loves her then—her joy—he goes to mother—send Honey out—Sara tries to help him, afraid being alone (Nancy in stateroom alone can face all her crimes proudly without fear—hell together will be heaven)—then Ethan, in spite of her evasions, forces mother to face truth in every aspect, crimes, fact he doesn't love Nancy but he will make her think he does by this—he finally gets her down to where she pleads, he can't ask her to—you love me!—remembers him as baby, have mercy—but he makes her judge him—

185

(when she says go away, don't tell me about it, do as you please, and he starts to go "all right, but I thought you would never forgive me if I didn't—And you're right, I never would) —At last she sends him out—"God damn honor of Harfords" —Honey comes back—get me drunk—I'll get drunk—I'll be a drunken peasant woman from this out—I'll tell honor of H[ar-fords]—and the honor of my lying drunken sponge of a father —to kiss my arse!" Honey comforts her, offers her drink—she dashes it out of his hand "And I a sodden coward like my father drunk afraid of life! I'll face it, I say—I'll face it with honor, like your father faced it God rest his soul!" (She collapses, weeping)—Ethan in Captain's room—takes Nancy's hand—"up those stairs?"—"Yes—that must be the way"— they go up—card game stops—Ethan "Goodbye, Wolfe—and to Honey when you see him"—Wolfe "Goodbye, Ethan, I understand." Leda starts up "Wait—You can't—no—what the hell am I saying—go on—get out of here—God bless you!" They go out, hand in hand. "We'll swim out together—until the fog lifts. And then the sea will be alight[?] with beauty forevermore—because you are[?] you, etc." (They disappear off rear in fog)—Graber "I've lost everything. Oh, thank God, thank God, every cent I stole for you, Leda. I've lost it all! I'm free!" "You're not rid of your conscience yet. Play him for me —all he's won against me" "No" "Then I'll play him. Here" Wolfe (agitatedly) "No. I don't want you" "been[?] playing for what you want—then you're a fake—or else you're afraid of yourself" "I'll play" No. Cut! Quick! Mine's a ten. Cut, coward! Let me see. The Queen of Hearts! My God, he's won me with the Queen of Hearts."—I'll give you back to Graber." Graber says No, I don't want her now. I can be boss[?] now, I'm free" Leda says "You think you can get rid of me, do you. Oh no, Wolfe. Never. I love you, you fool—can't you see I love you?" (Sara's cabin) She senses moment they go overboard from bow—leaps to her feet again "Ethan! My firstborn! etc

Curtain

Casa Genotta, June 9 '35

E[than] tells her no hell when she says hell with him heaven—only sea[?]—sleep each other's arms

186

Eugene O'Neill's set design for Act 1, Scene 2 [detail]
[Size of original: 4 x 6 cm.]

rough hewn beam ceiling

wood box   b(ack). p(orch).

chest d(rawers).

sea chest

wide 5 pane x
p(ane) windows

high backed bench

low rocker   cane-b(ack).

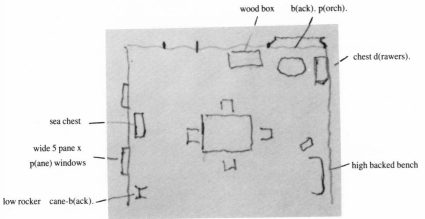

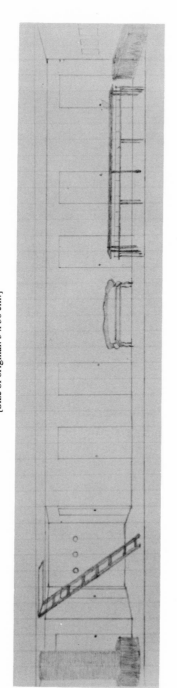

O'Neill's design for Act 2
[Size of original: 5 x 30 cm.]

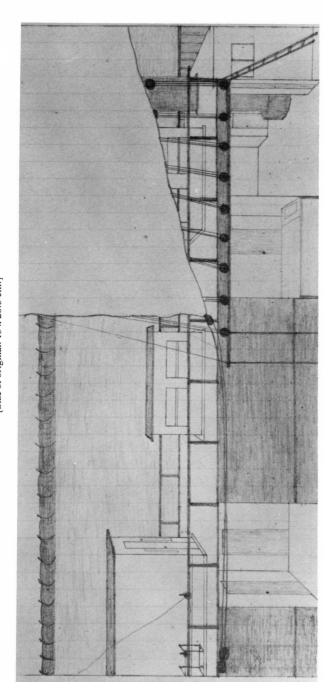

O'Neill's design for Act 3, Scene 2 [detail]
[Size of original: 13 x 26.5 cm.]

O'Neill's design for Act 3, Scene 1   [Size of original: 8.5 x 11 cm.]

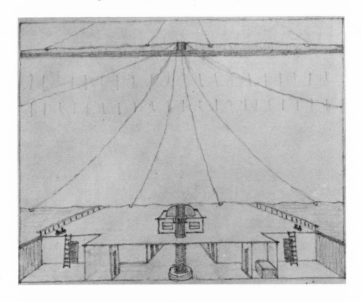

O'Neill's design for Act 4, Scene 1   [Size of original: 8.5 x 11 cm.]

Captain's cabin & sleeping room—
communicates with wheelhouse on
deck, so not necessary for him to enter
ladies' cabin

house contains dining salon & other
compartments

Skylight over pantry

helmsman in recess

entrance to captain's cabin . . .